CAREER

OF A

VETERINARIAN

*Thirty days behind the scenes
with a professional.*

GARDNER'S CAREER DIARIES™

CHRISTINE CALDER, D.V.M.

GARTH GARDNER COMPANY

GGC publishing

Washington DC, USA · London, UK

Editorial inquiries concerning this book should be mailed to: The Editor, Garth Gardner Company, 5107 13th Street N.W., Washington DC 20011 or e-mailed to: info@ggcinc.com.http://www.gogardner.com

ISBN-13: 978-1-58965-043-5

Library of Congress Cataloging-in-Publication Data

Calder, Christine.
  Career diary of a veterinarian: thirty days behind the scenes with a professional / Christine Calder.
      p. cm. -- (Gardner's career diaries)

  ISBN-13: 978-1-58965-043-5

  1. Calder, Christine--Diaries. 2. Veterinarians--United States--Diaries.
3. Veterinary medicine--Vocational guidance--United States. I. Title.
  SF613.C34A3 2007

  636.089092--dc22

                           2007049575

Printed in Canada

TABLE OF CONTENTS

ACKNOWLEDGMENTS

I'd like to dedicate this manuscript to my parents, who taught me that I could do anything in the world, even write a book. I would also like to acknowledge my husband and our children, who graciously put up with me as I took the time to write this. I extend my appreciation to my high school English teacher, Dr. Campbell, who encouraged me to write in the active rather than the passive voice. I've tried to do that, to the best of my ability. Finally, it's my intention to encourage anyone with an interest in veterinary medicine to pursue the dream. The animals will love you for it and, if I can do it, so can you.

BIOGRAPHY

My name is Christine Calder, and I work as a veterinarian at the Medomak Veterinary Practice in Waldoboro, Maine. My undergraduate major was animal science at Mississippi State University. My advanced degree was awarded in 1998, when I graduated from Mississippi State University College of Veterinary Medicine in Starkville, Mississippi.

Growing up along the New Jersey shore, I knew from my earliest school days that I wanted to be a veterinarian. In high school I doubled up on math and science courses to get a jump on any pre-veterinary classes I'd need to take in college. My high score on the ACT entrance exam gave me the recognition I needed for consideration in the Early Entry program at Mississippi State. I was one of fourteen students so recognized, which meant that the veterinary school would hold a space for me as long as I maintained a certain grade point average and took the appropriate classes. I entered veterinary school in 1994.

I married my husband during my freshman year of veterinary school, and my daughter was born during my junior year. After graduation, we moved back to New Jersey to be closer to my family and also because I received a job offer from one of the places where I'd previously worked as an intern. I remained with my first practice for a year, until my husband's employer transferred him to a location near Philadelphia. At that point we moved across the state to Woodbury, New Jersey. I continued to practice veterinary medicine as an associate and relief vet for the next eight years.

We moved to Maine in August 2006. I'm the mother of three children, ages 11, 9, and 2. We live on two acres outside Waldoboro along with five dogs, five cats, and a bearded dragon.

CURRENT POSITION AND RESPONSIBILITIES

The position of veterinarian involves many responsibilities to both patient and client. Upon graduating from veterinary school I took an oath that states, in part, "I will use my scientific knowledge and skills for the benefit of society through the protection of animal health and the relief of animal suffering, the conservation of animal resources, the promotion of public health, and the advancement of medical knowledge."

On a daily basis I promote public awareness and protect the health of pets through annual wellness checkups and first-time visits by new puppies and kittens. Among my tools are examinations, vaccinations, and a whole battery of tests—checking against heartworm and examining feces and urine. I take these opportunities to discuss with pet owners the importance of annual and bi-annual exams as well as blood tests to detect early disease processes. These visits represent the best time for clients to learn about parasite control and the dangers of zoonotic diseases, where afflictions can be passed from animals to humans. Because behavioral problems are one of the main reasons animals are euthanized or surrendered to shelters, I often discuss the behavioral characteristics of my patients. Early recognition of such problems can allow for more effective treatment before these situations escalate out of control.

Whenever sick patients visit me, I'm given the opportunity to relieve an animal's suffering. Whether an ear or bladder infection, a broken leg, or porcupine quills stuck into its body, someone's beloved pet is in pain and it's my obligation to properly diagnose and treat that animal so it will feel better. I'm also tasked with the responsibility of euthanasia for those animals that are in the greatest amount of pain. This is a privilege I do not take lightly.

My job also involves the advancement of my medical knowledge. I accomplish this every day by reading reference books and doing Internet research, seeking out sources to help me diagnose and treat problems. I'm also able to tap into the knowledge of other veterinarians in my practice as well as with specialists in internal medicine, neurology, and surgery, among other fields. I furthermore gain knowledge by taking continuing education classes and attending lectures at all levels—nationally, regionally, statewide, and locally. As a member of the American Veterinary Medical Association, I attend the annual conference as well as state-sponsored lectures and locally organized meetings, all in the interest of meeting the second part of the veterinarian's oath, which states, "I accept as a lifelong obligation the continual improvement of my professional knowledge and competence."

I've been in practice for close to 10 years, and I take pride and comfort in the fact that I learn something every day to improve my knowledge. This "something" comes in multiple forms. It could be the patience and open-mindedness necessary to hear both sides of a story without making assumptions or judgments. Occasionally it's the hug I get from a client after the loss of a special patient and friend. There are times when it involves reading an article or attending a lecture.

With knowledge comes competence, but this skill is also bolstered by self-confidence—built with each correct diagnosis and successful treatment, and even when a mistake is made. A veterinary career is a tough one but also highly rewarding, both personally and professionally. I love it!

RESUMÉ

EMPLOYMENT

2006–present
Medomak Veterinary Services, Waldoboro, Maine
Associate veterinarian
- Perform routine vaccinations
- Examine ill pets
- Perform surgery one day a week and as needed
- Cover all emergency duty

2002–2006
Larchmont Animal Hospital, Mount Laurel, New Jersey
Relief veterinarian
- Performed routine examinations
- Treated ill pets and referred to surgery as needed

2005–2006
Winslow Animal Hospital, Sicklerville, New Jersey
Associate veterinarian
- Performed routine examinations
- Treated ill pets and referred to surgery as needed

2002–2005
Bryan Animal Hospital, Mount Holly, New Jersey
Associate veterinarian
- Performed routine examinations
- Treated ill pets and referred to surgery as needed

2003
Camden County College, Blackwood, New Jersey
Adjunct Professor, Surgical Nursing II
- Instructed veterinary technician students to calculate drugs plus how to prep and assist during surgery
- Taught sterilization techniques, wound healing, surgical protocols, and the use of different suture materials

1999–2002
Gloucester County Veterinary Hospital, Sewell, New Jersey
Associate veterinarian
- Performed routine examinations
- Treated ill pets and referred to surgery as needed

1998–1999
Ocean County Veterinary Hospital, Lakewood, New Jersey
Associate veterinarian
- Adjusted to the process of becoming a veterinarian
- Performed limited surgeries under the direction of veteran doctors

EDUCATION

Majored in Animal Science, Mississippi State University, Starkville, Mississippi

Doctor of Veterinary Medicine (DVM), Mississippi State University College of Veterinary Medicine

MEMBERSHIPS & LICENSING

- Member of the Maine Veterinary Association and the American Veterinary Medical Association
- Licensed by the states of Maine and New Jersey

Day 1 *JANUARY 8*

PREDICTIONS
- *Provide multiple rabies vaccinations*
- *Solve a behavioral problem*

DIARY

This time of the year tends to be slow for the average veterinary practice. Around the holidays, people spend money on presents and enjoy time with their families. Beginning in January, there's a rush to obtain rabies vaccinations and new puppy and kitten exams, but things are generally quiet until spring. As with most states, residents of Maine are required to license their dogs in the township or municipality where they live. The deadline is at the end of January, so we see quite a few dogs brought in just for vaccinations.

I find that puppies and kittens are the best part of my job. I love their warm breath, soft fur, and compact size. Those first visits are filled with some of the most important details a pet owner can learn. When it comes to behavior, puppies and kittens are generally a blank slate when they enter their new home. They need to be shown what they can put in their mouths, where they should go to the bathroom, and how to play properly—just like humans. They need exercise and socialization to reduce fearful behavior and to fulfill their need to expend all that massive energy.

THIS IS THE ANESTHESIA MACHINE THAT WE
USE DURING SURGERY.

My first appointment today is a pleasant yellow Lab that
lives part of the year in Maine and spends the rest of the
time on Cape Cod in Massachusetts. He's due to receive
all his vaccines today but already had a complete physical
two months ago, back when I saw him to analyze his weird
behavior. His owner reported that one moment he was
fine and the next he'd act like a different dog, afraid of his
surroundings. It can be difficult to distinguish between a
medical and a behavioral problem, and it's often necessary
to rely on other diagnostic tests as well as a process of
elimination. A different veterinarian had recently performed
a blood test, and everything was normal. The owner
believed the behavior was more pronounced whenever
coyotes were heard howling. The dog's physical was normal
as well, so my bet was on a behavioral reaction. Today the
client tells me that everything has been good since their last
visit, with no further episodes. It must have been the coyotes
that caused him to act so strangely.

VIEW FROM THE SURGERY WINDOW. WHICH I
FIND VERY CALMING.

A dog by the name of Sandals is my nine o'clock
appointment, due for her vaccinations as well as a full exam.
While checking her mouth I notice she has a fair amount of
dental disease. This is one of the most common infectious
diseases I see in dogs and cats. I suggest a daily brushing
regimen, but her owner doesn't think she can provide that.
Instead we agree on a full ultrasonic cleaning for later, and I
send her home with something to put in the dog's water to
reduce gingivitis and tarter buildup.

Sly is a lovable one-year-old cat, found near my client's
house. After gradually gaining the cat's trust, the new
owner was finally able to lure him into her home. The cat
has begun to show signs of an upper respiratory infection.
These are common in cats, especially those that were
strays, and are caused by a multitude of different viruses
or bacteria—the most common is the feline herpes virus.

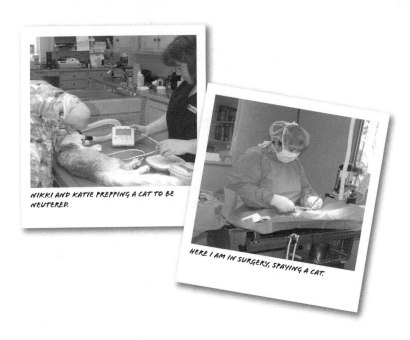

NIKKI AND KATIE PREPPING A CAT TO BE NEUTERED.

HERE I AM IN SURGERY, SPAYING A CAT.

Upon examination I find that the cat has gingivitis as well as conjunctivitis in both eyes. I also test him for feline leukemia (FeLV) and feline AIDS (FIV), since these diseases can lower a cat's immune response. Both tests show negative. I send him home with antibiotics and some ointment for his eyes.

My last appointment of the morning is a sick one. Patches is a five-year-old black-and-white cat with a history of crying at odd times. He has a long history of constipation and is currently taking medication for that condition. Last Thursday's exam showed a large amount of fecal matter in his colon, so I suggested that his owner increase the dosage temporarily to see if the stool would evacuate on its own. That did not happen. On Friday he returned to be radiographed, which revealed a lot of stool in his colon. The warm, soapy enema I administered didn't do the trick, which meant we had to sedate him and remove the material manually. He recovered well and returned home, but today he's back because his owner is worried that he's not urinating. One feel of his bladder tells me he must be urinating somewhere, so I send him home again. We reduce the frequency of his medication to twice a day, believing the current discomfort is likely due to cramps induced by the higher dosage.

After lunch it's time for Cocoa, a cute kitten who's here for her booster shots. In our practice, all cats receive a series of vaccinations until they're twelve weeks old. These vaccines protect against feline viral rhinothracheitis, panleukopenia, and calicivirus. Cocoa is here to receive her FVRCP booster and rabies shot today. This completes her booster series, but she'll be back in two months to be spayed.

The owner of Peanut, a 15-year-old dog, brings her in and reports she believes the dog may have suffered a stroke. On several occasions over the weekend Peanut reportedly couldn't stand up. She also suffered from diarrhea and seemed generally uncomfortable. In the examining room she has trouble breathing and does not like me touching her belly. A blood test shows a very high white blood cell count, which tells me she's working to fight off an infection, while a radiograph series highlights either a tumor in her abdomen or evidence of pancreatitis. The owners elect to hospitalize her to see how she does overnight. We admit her, provide some pain medicine, and then begin intravenous fluids.

LESSONS/PROBLEMS
Staying on schedule wasn't too difficult today. I was able to see all my appointments and still make it home by dinner. I hope I'll have better news for Peanut's owner tomorrow.

THIS IS WHERE THE CAT CARRIERS GO FOR STORAGE WHEN THE CATS BOARD OR COME IN FOR SURGERY.

Day 2 JANUARY 9

PREDICTIONS
- Check on yesterday's hospital admission
- Spay a dog and neuter two cats
- See a sick ferret

DIARY
Today is my on-call day. Our clinic shares around-the-clock emergency duty with three other local hospitals. I'm assigned to this job every Tuesday, beginning at 8:00 a.m. and continuing for the subsequent 24 hours. Tuesdays tend to be quiet as far as emergency calls go, but there have been times when I've come in as late as midnight and as early as five in the morning. The first thing I do upon arrival is check on Peanut. She's showing a great deal of discomfort,

for which I give her another pain injection. After explaining the circumstances to her owner, the woman makes the difficult decision to euthanize Peanut. She wants to say her final good-byes, so we'll hold off taking any action until she arrives later this morning.

We have three surgeries on today's docket. Pets scheduled for elective surgery are admitted between 8:00 a.m. and 8:30 a.m. daily. It's a fairly light day, with one dog spay and two cat neuters. The cats will be up first, since this procedure takes only about 10 minutes to perform. All three clients today have opted out of pre-surgical blood work, which speeds up the process but makes the operations more risky. We recommend this work to make sure the pet's organs are healthy enough to handle anesthesia. People often decline this service due to financial constraints.

After the neutering, Peanut's owners come in to say farewell. They spend some time with her before I euthanize her. The dog is happy to see them, but she's clearly weak. I assure them they're making the right decision and then I help her pass away quietly. They elect to take her home and bury her there.

Finally it's time for the spaying, known in the vet world as an ovario-hysterectomy. Dina is a beautiful six-month-old chocolate lab. We gave her a tranquilizer when she was admitted, but now it's time for IV anesthesia. She's surprisingly calm and we're able to intubate her easily. During the prep for surgery I notice a skin infection on her belly, so I call her owner. After reassuring him that everything's going well, he tells me they've had a major flea problem over the last few months. That explains her skin issues. He approves us to apply Frontline®, and I'll send the dog home on antibiotics. Her surgery proceeds without complication.

My afternoon starts up again at four o'clock with more routine wellness exams and vaccinations. But one appointment proves especially interesting. I'm scheduled for a re-check on Rudy, a ferret I saw last week. He's having trouble moving his hind end and isn't eating well. Last week he came in wheezing and with discharge from his nose, plus his temperature was 104 degrees. That's very high for a ferret. Last year he exhibited similar clinical signs. At that point we ran blood work and placed him on antibiotics, which helped him to improve. Since he responded so well with that line of treatment, this time around we began with the antibiotics to see what happens. Rudy is back today because he's still not walking, although his appetite is much better. It's possible he has insulinoma. This is a relatively common disease in ferrets, especially with older ones. It can affect a ferret's blood sugar level, making them weak in the hind end. We decide to do some blood work. His glucose is actually high rather than low. This rules out insulinoma but doesn't explain his weak hind end. Rudy's temperature is still high at 103 degrees, so we decide to continue with antibiotics. We'll radiograph Rudy's abdomen and hips if he fails to improve.

After several more routine appointments my aunt brings in her dog, Conner. He's here primarily for a rabies vaccination, but we have a problem to diagnose as well. He's been scratching himself raw over the past few months. His initial response to steroids and antibiotics was favorable, but now his scratching has returned with a vengeance. I'm able to examine him, but he's clearly not happy to see the vet as his warning growls show. Even with that, I'm able to get a good look at his skin. I find a flea and notice how red the spot is beneath it. My diagnosis is some type of allergy, with fleas being the most likely culprit. My aunt will need to institute continuous flea control and give him the medicine I prescribe. If his skin problems persist, we'll go to a special diet and possibly institute stricter environmental controls. I give him his rabies shot and send him on his way, offering to make a house call the next time Conner needs an exam. My aunt lives 45 minutes away, and perhaps the familiar surroundings will eliminate the dog's growling issue.

LESSONS/PROBLEMS

It's possible to see problems with fleas, even in the dead of a Maine winter. With the euthanasia today, I'm reminded that the best thing to do may involve letting go rather than holding on.

PREDICTIONS

- *Attend an office meeting*
- *Examine a vomiting cat*
- *Diagnose a pug with allergies*

DIARY

My first appointment has canceled, which works out well since our receptionist tells me this client has been difficult to please in the past. Ever since I was 10 years old I knew I wanted to be a veterinarian. All my grade-school projects and book reports were geared toward veterinary medicine, and I spent four years of high school sitting in math and science classes to prepare myself for college and acceptance into veterinary school. I simply never bothered to factor in the people. When I took my first job, I suddenly learned that being a vet was perhaps more about the people than the animals. Not one of my veterinary medicine courses prepared me for the human element I'd encounter every day. My four-legged patients are often an extension of the client. The client controls the money, which then controls what you can do to help the animal. It's a tangled web, and veterinarians oftentimes find themselves worrying more about what the client can afford than what's best for the animal. We learn at conferences not to judge or predetermine what our clients can afford or will choose to do. We're also taught to offer every possible option and allow the client to make the final decision. This works

THE BABY SCALE THAT WE WEIGH ANIMALS UNDER 20LBS. IT IS PORTABLE.

THIS DOG MOBILE HANGS IN THE WAITING ROOM, ABOVE THE ENTRANCE TO OUR CLINIC.

well most of the time, but you quickly learn that you can't save them all. Sometimes you're left without a confirmed diagnosis, which can be frustrating.

Because animals can't speak for themselves, owners come up with their own interpretation of what's wrong with their animal. They may even do a layman's diagnosis and attempt treatment. Today I see a perfect example of that. A client comes in with her five-year-old dachshund she had accidentally burned on one ear. The woman applied tea tree oil to the wound over the past week, thinking it would heal. I use clippers to trim away the hair and see what's going on.

THE SMALL-DOG WALKING AREA IN THE REAR OF THE CLINIC. IT IS ENTIRELY FENCED IN.

There is a great deal of pus and the skin has simply sloughed away. In short, the area looks horrible. When confronted with the evidence the woman says, "I thought I had it under control." My reply is brief and a bit sad. "You need antibiotics, and that's going to scar," I say.

My 10 o'clock appointment is a perfect example of the consequences of financial limitations. Gray, a two-year-old orange-and-white domestic shorthair cat, was presented as ADR. That's vet shorthand for the catch-all complaint, "Ain't Doin' Right." We use that acronym a lot around here. He's been vomiting for the past two days. The owner can't say if he has diarrhea because he's an outdoor cat and does not use a litterbox. My physical exam is unremarkable, which is good. I'd prefer to do a radiograph to search for a foreign body, plus run blood work to determine possible signs of

THE BENCH IN EXAM ROOM 3 WHERE THE
CLIENTS SIT. SOMETIMES DOGS(AND CATS)
LIKE TO HIDE UNDER THE BENCHES, AND IT
CAN BE HARD TO GET THEM OUT.

toxicity by examining liver and kidney values. Gray's owner can't afford to run all these tests right now, so she opts instead for a bland diet and a de-worming. She promises to return if he fails to improve. I'm left hoping that worms are his only problem.

Minnie is here to have her anal glands expressed. I don't mind doing this, but it sure is a smelly process. There are two small glands that sit just inside the rectum. Some dogs and cats need them drained regularly because the animal can't do it effectively on its own. Poor diet and irregular bowel movements are one reason for this affliction, but it can also be caused by allergies. In Minnie's case it's allergies, although we haven't yet determined what this dog happens to be allergic to.

Lunchtime today is taken up by an office meeting. Once

a month we close from noon to two o'clock and meet collaboratively to discuss business affairs or attend an educational session put on by a representative from one of the pharmaceutical companies—more commonly known as drug reps. Today we're discussing a wide variety of subjects. Our office manager and the clinic's owner will attend a veterinary conference in Florida. When the owner returns to town, she'll look after our job evaluations. Puppies are chewing on the drawer knobs in the exam rooms and we need to figure out how to stop that behavior, especially when the owners aren't helping. Finally, each of us will receive $50 to donate to our favorite charity. We're advised to consider our choice now before the sign-up sheet is passed around. The meeting ends with presents and a cake for the two January birthday celebrants, which includes me.

After lunch I examine a black Lab named Black Jack. He has a number of small lumps under his skin, which is common in older dogs, but one on his leg has grown at an alarming rate. I decide to take an aspirate to look for malignant cells, which means I'll use a hypodermic needle to remove a few cells from the center of the mass and examine them under a microscope. Black Jack's aspirate is not good. I see many cells with more than one nucleus, an abnormality that ultimately leads to malignancy. Treatment options include surgery with chemotherapy or radiation, or amputation, or close monitoring followed by euthanasia when the disease no longer proves manageable. His owners believe he's not a good candidate for amputation due to arthritis, and they're not interested in chemical therapy. Instead they'll keep him as comfortable as possible for as long as they can.

LESSONS/PROBLEMS

There's more psychology involved in veterinary medicine than most people think. When colleagues at a vet clinic work together as a team, we do a much better job for our clients and patients. Regular office meetings and team-building exercises are an important part of that effort.

Day 4 JANUARY 12

PREDICTIONS

- *Work alone while others are out of town at a conference*
- *Examine a dog recently experiencing seizures*

DIARY

Today starts my very first week alone as the only doctor in the hospital as well as my weekend on call for the month of January. My boss and our office manager leave today for the North American Veterinary Conference in Orlando, Florida. There are numerous conferences across the country, where veterinarians gather to earn continuing education credits by attending lectures. There are also exhibitors to visit, with people selling everything from photos for your waiting room walls to the latest diagnostic equipment. It's a great opportunity to learn all about the new products on the market.

Daisy is a four-year-old beagle that had her first seizure a week ago. The physical exam shows nothing remarkable, so I explain the various causes of seizure to the owner. These include liver disease, ingestion of something toxic, a brain tumor, or epilepsy. I recommend blood work to rule out some of the causes as well as to establish a baseline for future reference. The owner agrees, and all the readings come up normal. Since the dog's last seizure was a week ago, I suggest that her owner watch closely and keep a log of further incidents. If the seizures become more frequent

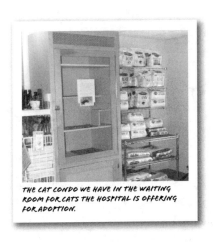

THE CAT CONDO WE HAVE IN THE WAITING ROOM FOR CATS THE HOSPITAL IS OFFERING FOR ADOPTION.

or intense, I'll consider prescribing some anti-seizure medication.

While at lunch I get an urgent call to return to the office. A new client will bring in the family's cat that was attacked by a raccoon in the middle of the day. Rabies is my immediate concern. Rabies is a fatal disease that affects all mammals. It's most common in wild animals such as raccoons, skunks, and bats, but recently we've found it in cats, and even a cow tested positive not too long ago. Anyone working in animal medicine is vaccinated against the disease in veterinary school, but the general public is not. People who are exposed to rabies undergo a series of four booster shots to prevent infection, we hope. Things become more complicated when pets have not been vaccinated, as is the case with this feline. Boots arrives in the company of a husband and wife, and their two-year-old daughter. I'm told the cat was in their yard when a raccoon came out of nowhere and began attacking the cat. They were able to scare off the raccoon but could not catch it. Neither the man nor the woman can say for certain when Boots had her most recent rabies shot, speculating that it may have been 10 years ago or so. They had used gloves to handle the cat, which was a smart move. Boots appears alert and responsive, but she shows multiple bite wounds on her ankles and there is saliva on her neck. Our receptionist and I are the only rabies-vaccinated people in the building, so she holds the cat while I do the exam. I clip the hair from around the wounds, wash them with an anti-bacterial scrub, and administer a rabies shot. We discuss options the family faces. I explain it's highly unusual for a raccoon to be out in the middle of the day and to attack a cat for no reason. I also outline the threat to them and their need to seek medical advice, since rabies can be spread to humans. Our next move is to place Boots into quarantine. She will be kept in an escape-proof room in the house at all times, never leaving except under direct supervision and control of an adult. It may take up to six months to see any clinical signs associated with rabies, so we discuss euthanasia as an option. However, the family believes they can keep her confined to a room where she will be safe and happy throughout the quarantine period. These cases can be difficult because of the risk to clients as well as to hospital personnel, but rabies is not the only zoonotic disease—meaning transmittable to humans—we worry about in veterinary hospitals. Leptospirosis is a bacterial disease transmitted through urine, plus there are parasites such as roundworms or sarcoptic mange, and fungal infections such as ringworm. Being a veterinarian can be a high-risk job.

After Boots, it's time to see Page a three-year-old yellow Labrador that ate a whole bag of bagels. Normally I would not be too concerned, but Page is lethargic and there were raisins in the bagels. Raisins and grapes are two new emerging toxicities we see in dogs. These two fruits have been linked to kidney failure, and it only takes a few raisins or grapes to cause a problem. We draw some blood to check her kidney and liver functions. Everything comes back normal, which is good. I send her home to be watched closely for signs of vomiting or diarrhea.

After Page there are no more scheduled appointments, so I take advantage of the situation and head home for the evening. But sure enough, I soon get a call that requires me to head back. It's a client from one of the other hospitals. Their dog, Bubba, received a rabies vaccination this afternoon and is now very lethargic and he feels warm. My physical shows that he is a little unsteady on his feet, but his temperature is normal and he is bright, alert, and responsive. I send him home with an anti-inflammatory and instruct his owners to call me if they have any more problems during the night.

Emergency duty is tough on me. When I worked in New Jersey, we had a round-the-clock emergency clinic within a 20-minute drive, plus a major teaching hospital just across the bridge in Philadelphia. In Maine, the dynamics are different. The closest 24-hour clinic is in Portland, 90 minutes away. Emergencies are learning experiences, but they can be an inconvenience as well. I'm not crazy about leaving my house in the middle of the night or going into the office alone to meet a stranger. When the pager goes off, you never know what the situation will be. For instance, this evening I received a call from a client who told me his dog just died. There's nothing I can do other than lend a sympathetic ear and help suggest burial arrangements.

LESSONS/PROBLEMS

Today I began a week alone without any senior backup. It's important for pet owners to vaccinate their animals against rabies and show extreme care when confronted with wildlife, especially in their own backyards.

PREDICTIONS

- *See a Sheltie for a second opinion on his nose*
- *Examine a dog that's suffering a bloody nose*
- *Rule out Lyme disease in a limping dog*

DIARY

At this practice I work every other Saturday, generally a very busy day for us. Sick dogs and cats may have shown signs of illness for several days, but it's suddenly important for them to be examined today because their owners are off work. That can make a four-hour day seem a lot longer. We begin the day with three open appointments, but by 9:30 a.m. we're squeezing everyone in. My early appointments involve only vaccination boosters, which are simple to do, but at half past ten I'm asked to provide a second opinion. Clients make second-opinion appointments for a variety of reasons. Sometimes they're unhappy with their existing doctor, or they may be frustrated because one or more treatment options have failed to improve their pet's health. In other instances, it's because they don't like the diagnosis that's been made and they're hoping to hear something different elsewhere. Bear is a Sheltie with a sore on his nose that has refused to heal. The other veterinarian had already performed the appropriate preliminary diagnostics, which included a skin scraping, a fungal test, and even a thyroid profile. This makes my life easier but also leaves me with few options on where to go next. Because it's only been two

WE ARE BOXING DOWN A CAT TO GIVE HIM A LION CUT. WE USE THIS TYPE OF ANESTHESIA INDUCTION FOR HARD-TO-HANDLE ANIMALS.

days since his last visit, I recommend patience and some local antibiotic cream until the thyroid results come back. Bear's owner seems pleased with this course of action.

My next appointment proves a bit more challenging, limited as I am by the owner's finances. A dog named Baby has been here several times over the past two months for excessive sneezing, which two weeks ago began to produce nosebleeds. At the time I discussed allergies, tick-borne diseases, various bleeding disorders, and the possibility of a tumor. The owner has tried antihistamines but can't afford additional diagnostics. The antihistamines worked briefly, but now the bleeding is worse. At a minimum I'd like to do a tick serology, a complete blood count and radiography, warning that nasal tumors don't always show up under x-rays. Patients like Baby often need a rhinoscopy—an endoscope slipped deep into the nose—to really see what's going on. The woman says she'd prefer euthanasia because she can't afford the diagnostics. I'm not prepared to do that, so I offer an alternative. Due to the dog's age and the fact that the bleeding comes from only one nostril, I suspect we're dealing with a nasal tumor. We place Baby on Piroxicam, an anti-inflammatory helpful in shrinking some tumors, for whatever reason. We'll see if this does the trick.

My last appointment of the day is Teddy, an overweight five-year-old Shetland sheepdog. Apparently Teddy has been limping for three weeks. Yesterday a friend told the owner it had to be Lyme disease, since that person's dog also limped and was diagnosed with it. As a result, Teddy's owner rushes him right over to us. During my exam I fail to find any swelling or pain in the joints, which are clear indicators for Lyme. The dog favors one front leg when he walks but is not running a fever. I run a Lyme test for peace of mind, and the results are negative. I place Teddy on Rimadyl and stress to the owner the importance that he lose ten pounds—the dog, not the man. I suspect the dog has arthritis, and the extra weight is probably aggravating this condition.

After returning home a bit past one o'clock, I receive a frantic call from a man whose 12-year-old dog is having trouble breathing. While I'm taking the pet's history over the phone, the owner reports that the breathing seems to have improved. Just the same, I recommend we see the dog immediately. He lives 40 minutes from my clinic but only 20 minutes from his regular clinic, which will be open again at two o'clock. Rather than coming to see us, I suggest he start for his usual place right away.

Responding to calls from regular clients of other veterinary hospitals is challenging. Treatment histories are not available online and there's no direct link to the other hospital's records, so obtaining a clear history on an animal is difficult. In emergency medicine, I've learned that having a good history is vital to triaging a pet. You have to learn how to ask the right questions, and it takes time to develop that skill.

LESSONS/PROBLEMS

Pet owners who find it difficult to afford specific diagnoses or treatments can make it very difficult on a vet to make the correct call on what's ailing the animal. Clients who place emergency calls don't always have the answers at their fingertips when it comes to their animal's history. It would be great if we could have real-time access to past treatments and a list of vaccinations.

PREDICTIONS

- *Spend Sunday on call, waiting for emergencies to crop up*

DIARY

Today is Sunday and, at nine o'clock, my pager begins to chirp—two calls in a row. One concerns a cat that hasn't urinated in the past 24 hours and appears quite uncomfortable. The other call is about an older cocker spaniel that is showing general discomfort. The cat needs to be seen because I'm concerned about urinary blockage. However, the cocker spaniel's owner hesitates because he's not sure he wants to pay the emergency fee. I head to the office to meet up with the cat's owners, and meanwhile I check with my assistant and put her on standby notice. I'd prefer not to call her in unless absolutely necessary, since it will cost the client an additional fee if I have to bring in help.

As I had feared, Rudy the cat has a distended bladder that I'm unable to express. He experienced this problem a few months ago as well. The first thing I do following my brief exam is to provide the owners with a price of treatment up front. I've learned the hard way to address this issue immediately. Several months ago a dog was brought in to have a laceration repaired. The wound was obviously old and I found it necessary to install several drains to help alleviate the infection. Since the wound was badly infected, I put him on two different antibiotics to clear things up. The owners were very angry at the cost of treatment and refused to pay the bill. They explained they would have euthanized him had they known it was going to cost so much, since he was "just a dog." It's now my policy to provide an estimate to every client I see.

Rudy's owners are not happy with the cost of the prospective treatment. When they brought him to his regular veterinarian for the same problem a few months ago, the fee was much lower, I'm told. I explain that I'm interested in broadening the treatment, since this is the second time in less than three months he's had this problem. They decline everything except what's necessary for immediate treatment. I try to explain that without blood work, urinalysis, and a radiograph, there is no guarantee he'll improve, or that we would even have a baseline for reference to detect any improvement. They agree to take that risk.

While I'm in the examining room with Rudy and his owners, my pager goes off again. Emma, a young female cat in heat, was outdoors when she got into a nasty fight. I invite them to come right over, since I'm already at the hospital. While I'm waiting for Emma, the gentleman with the cocker spaniel shows up at the door. The dog appears to be in pain and doesn't even want to take one step into the clinic. I discover she has a problem in her neck so I offer to run a radiograph, which the owner declines. At that point I prescribe an anti-inflammatory, and the client has muscle relaxants from a previous visit to his regular veterinarian.

NIKKI IS CLEANING THE TEETH OF A LITTLE YORKIE.

Emma arrives at noon. She has a bite wound on her head and suffers from a scratched cornea. I discuss the likelihood that she has been impregnated as well. I administer a rabies shot for her bite wound of unknown origin and order her placed into quarantine. Her owner will immediately consider spaying her.

After taking care of Emma and Rudy, my pager is silent until half past five. A woman calls about her female Westie, which delivered a pup three days ago via C-section. The owner is quite distraught because the puppy just died and the mother has been vomiting. After posing several questions, I discover that the female dog saw her regular veterinarian yesterday, where she underwent radiography and blood work. Everything came up normal. I advise the woman to halt the medications and see if the vomiting stops while also offering to see her first as an emergency. She tells me she's already left a message for her regular vet and is awaiting a return call. Conversations like these make me wonder why they call, even though I know it's just to be reassured.

LESSONS/PROBLEMS
Whenever I'm on call on a Sunday, it's almost guaranteed that I'll end up at the clinic. Discussing the cost of treatment before giving it allows a pet owner to decide on a course of action that fits within their budget.

THIS IS ERIN AND AMY. ERIN IS AN ASSISTANT AND AMY IS A RECEPTIONIST.

Day 7 *JANUARY 15*

PREDICTIONS

- *See a Jack Russell terrier that may have been poisoned*
- *Check over a dog that has experienced significant weight loss*
- *Run diagnostics on an anemic cat*

DIARY

Snow is in the forecast. Even though it's eight o'clock and we've seen very little accumulation, our phones are ringing off the hook with people calling to cancel their appointments. When I lived in New Jersey, people often panicked at the first sign of snow and everything shut down. Somehow I expected it to be different in Maine, but I didn't factor in the hilly terrain and how treacherous the roads can be with a mere dusting of snow on the ground. The fact that most highways are not plowed until the storm is over is yet another mitigating factor. By 8:30 a.m. the snow is really coming down. We decide to move all our afternoon appointments to the morning and close early. Most people are happy to accommodate us since they'd just as soon not be out in the bad weather.

After several routine vaccinations, I see a one-year-old Jack Russell terrier named Scooby. The owner has brought her in because the dog licked a snow shovel and vomited several times this morning. The owner reports no other recent difficulties. As I prepare to examine Scooby, she's bouncing around my office and bares her teeth as if she's prepared to bite me. I'm unable to find anything wrong during the physical exam, so I offer to run blood work that would check out her kidney and liver values. Instead, her owner elects to take the dog home and watch her closely. I'm fairly certain Scooby will be fine. People often fear their dog has been poisoned when it behaves strangely, especially when vomiting is involved, but I find that's rarely the case.

My next appointment is with an old pointer named Sam. He's lost close to 30 pounds since we last saw him three months ago. That's a lot of weight to drop in so short a time, even for a big dog like Sam that used to weigh in the neighborhood of 130 pounds. Other than his arthritis, I find no significant negative clinical signs. His gums look a little pale to me and I don't like his weight loss, so we decide to run some blood work. It will take a while to get the results, so I send Sam and his owner home and promise to call as soon as I know the outcome.

With the snow coming down hard and sticking to the highway, I'm grateful we have only a few more appointments before I can go home. I see two animals for booster vaccines and then it's my last appointment of the day. Tabby is a cat we saw a few weeks ago. He was so sick that I wasn't sure he'd make it through the night. When I ran his blood work, he showed up with such severe anemia that he needed a transfusion. Since he's only three years old my first thought was feline leukemia, an autoimmune disease, or else hemobartonella, which is feline infectious anemia. I tested him for FeLV and FIV, both of which came up negative. We subsequently chose a course of therapy that included Prednisone and antibiotics. He responded extremely well and started to eat again almost immediately. Today is his final recheck. We were able to taper him off the Prednisone a few weeks ago, and last week was his final dose of antibiotics. Today his blood work shows normal, so I give him a clean bill of health and send him home after giving him his overdue rabies shot.

I'm told that Sam's blood work is finished, and the news is not good. It appears his kidneys are failing. In older dogs there are many things that cause this, but we often don't find out the actual reason unless we do an autopsy. These are the hardest phone calls to make. No one wants to hear that an animal they love may soon die. I call Sam's owner, offering to run additional diagnostics to see if there's anything we can treat, such as an infection. However, the family decides they'll do their best to keep him comfortable and let nature take its course. They'll be back for euthanasia when he starts vomiting or stops eating.

LESSONS/PROBLEMS

Snow brings on cancelled appointments. As a veterinarian, telling someone their animal has a terminal illness is one of the most difficult aspects of this job.

Day 8 *JANUARY 16*

- *Perform a dental procedure on a cat*
- *Check out a limping cocker spaniel*
- *Re-examine a dog with a corneal ulcer*

DIARY

Today is my day for surgery. In my second year at Mississippi State University CVM, we divided up into groups of three and would spend one day a week in surgery, each taking turns as the surgeon, the anesthesiologist, and the assistant. Most of the work we performed involved spays and neuters on animals from shelters, but there were also bone labs and cadaver labs to learn how to fix fractures and ligament damage.

During my first year of practice, I was not assigned a set surgical day. Because of that, my surgical skills were rudimentary. At my next practice, staffed by three vets—one of whom did no surgery at all—I was able to gain much more experience. Not until my third position, however, and in my fifth year of private practice did I truly become comfortable with surgery. It was there that I learned how to do a cystotomy—bladder stone surgery—and foreign body removal. I also taught surgical skills to veterinary technicians, running three labs a week at the local shelter. The technicians anesthetized and prepped the animals, and then assisted me while I performed the procedures. This is

EXAM ROOM 2, WHERE WE SEE ALL OF THE EYE CASES AND LOOK AT RADIOGRAPHS.

the experience that boosted my confidence, because I did the surgery alone while teaching others at the same time. Because of this class I became a true surgeon.

Our schedule today is fairly light, with a dog spay and a cat neutering. Also, one of our technicians has brought in his cat for dental cleaning. Everything goes smoothly until the dental. Gary the kitty won't stay asleep, so we monitor him closely through the anesthesia machine. When an animal does not easily reach a steady state of anesthesia, it's a nerve-racking situation for the technician as well as for the veterinarian. We're constantly on the edge of our seats to make sure nothing goes wrong. All this attention apparently pays off, as Gary makes it through fine. We breathe much easier when he revives.

My first exam of the day is a new patient. Nellie is an older cocker spaniel that has been limping on her right hind leg for a few days. Upon palpating it I detect something called "drawer" in her knee. This is a sign that she ruptured her cranial cruciate ligament. This type of knee injury is fairly common in dogs, often occurring when chasing after squirrels or some other moving target. We call it a sports injury because football players also suffer from it. Nellie's owner has administered Metacam, which is an NSAID or non-steroidal anti-inflammatory. I advise her to continue with this but also report the dog will probably need surgery to repair the damage. I recommend a series of radiographs to rule out any other causes of her sudden lameness. Nellie's owners love her but don't have the money right now to pursue further diagnostics or treatment. I feel badly for Nellie, but she's a smaller dog so I hope the Metacam will relieve her pain until the knee heals on its own. If she doesn't improve, her owners promise they'll find the funding for surgery.

Next is Katie, a 13-year-old Chesapeake Bay retriever with a non-healing corneal ulcer. We saw her last week and placed her on a triple-antibiotic ointment. She has returned for a follow-up visit. I stain the eye and see that the ulcer has not improved. This can happen in older dogs, where advanced age causes a delay in healing. I decide to change her antibiotics from the ointment to an eye drop called Tobramycin, designed for humans. I warn her owner that it will take time and patience to heal the eye, and we'll recheck it again next week.

Before I leave the office for the day, my emergency pager sounds. I ring back the caller, who owns a four-year-old Doberman. They were at another clinic today, where the dog underwent local anesthesia to have a growth removed. They fed him shortly after he returned home from the hospital and now he's acting oddly—clearly unable to get comfortable and continually trying to vomit. They also report that his stomach looks distended. I suggest they proceed immediately to the emergency clinic in Portland. Their dog may have bloat. This serious condition occasionally turns up after surgery, where the stomach has twisted and impeded the flow of blood. Other organs are often involved as well. Clinical signs include a distended stomach, abdominal pain, and non-productive vomiting. This must be treated surgically, and the post-operative period calls for careful monitoring. We can't help because we're not a 24-hour staffed hospital, but the emergency clinic in Portland has this capability. They will be in good hands down there.

LESSONS/PROBLEMS
Maintaining a steady state of anesthesia can be difficult, and constant monitoring of the patient is vital. Corneal ulcers need time and patience to heal. Some emergencies are best referred to a round-the-clock hospital for care.

PREDICTIONS

- *Treat a cat with chronic diarrhea*
- *See an older dog with possible cognitive dysfunction*
- *Recheck a dog recovering from cruciate ligament surgery*

DIARY

My day begins with a no-show appointment for a cat needing radiographs and a cystocentesis. This procedure involves inserting a needle directly into the bladder to obtain a sterile urine sample. Veterinarians use this technique for urine culture and sensitivities for bladder infections, as well as for those animals that won't give us a free-catch sample. Spook was scheduled because she has a recurring bladder infection, despite undergoing two separate stints of antibiotics. I'll look for bladder stones and we'll also culture her urine to make sure she's on the right antibiotics. Her owners cancel this appointment shortly before she was scheduled to arrive, claiming they believe she's better.

My next appointment is Daisy, a cat adopted out of our hospital many years ago. She was found at the side of the road, covered in fleas and loaded with parasites. We nursed her back to health but also found it necessary to perform two surgeries on her for rectal prolapse. This condition occurs when a cat or dog has severe diarrhea. Daisy is here today because she's started losing weight and her diarrhea has returned with a vengeance. She refuses to use her litterbox and is not eating properly. Her blood work is normal, so we test her feces for intestinal parasites. When that test comes back normal as well, I decide to prescribe an antibiotic called Metronidazole. She's already on a limited-ingredient diet, which has worked so far to control the diarrhea. Her owner agrees to call me in a few days to let me know if this new medication is helping.

Cassidy is next, an older beagle that started barking at her owner for no apparent reason. This extremely overweight dog has a history of urinary tract infections, underactive thyroid, and arthritis. Cassidy's physical shows significant clues to her barking. I explain to her owner that Cassidy's behavior may result from frustration with her inability to move around comfortably. It's potentially a sign of early onset cognitive dysfunction, but the dog seems fairly alert for that condition. I recommend exercise and a change in diet to get her to lose some weight, and we should recheck her thyroid to make sure the medication is at its proper dosage. It's also possible she has another urinary infection and was barking to go outside, but could not stand up easily to head for the door. Her owner offers to bring in a urine sample for testing, and she'll observe Cassidy's behavior more closely to see if there are further clues as to why she keeps barking at family members.

My next appointment is Jenny, an 18-month-old Newfoundland the owners obtained from a rescue shelter. She's been acting uncomfortably for the past week, showing a reluctance to stand up and lie down. Her appetite has also

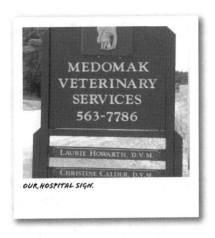

OUR HOSPITAL SIGN.

decreased. During the physical her knees feel thick to me, and she has discomfort in her hips as well as her right elbow. I recommend blood work to see if she has any underlying reason for this lack of appetite. Her blood work is normal, so we put Jenny on an anti-inflammatory regimen and schedule a visit next week for radiography under sedation.

Petey comes in for a recheck after his cruciate surgery three weeks ago. We've asked his owner to bring in the dog earlier than his previously scheduled appointment. Even though his owner reports Petey did well shortly after surgery when putting weight on his good leg, over the past few days he hasn't wanted to move at all. I place Petey on the examination table and immediately recognize the problem— he's ruptured the cruciate ligament in his good leg. This is an unfortunate complication of cruciate surgery because the dog is forced to put all of its weight on the good hind leg while the injured leg heals. Sometimes the knee can't handle the additional pressure, and that cruciate ligament ruptures. He'll need additional surgery, which is expensive and inconvenient for the owner. We decide to give Petey more time, examining him again in six weeks. If he still favors his good leg we'll operate, since his recently healed leg will be strong enough by then to support his weight. Fortunately, once a damaged cruciate ligament is repaired, it can't rupture a second time.

LESSONS/PROBLEMS

Anorexia can be a subtle sign that indicates another problem such as pain. If one cruciate ligament undergoes surgical repair, there's a risk the one in the good leg may rupture during recovery.

PREDICTIONS

- See two puppies for their first vaccinations
- Check over one of my assistant's dogs
- Examine a new patient for a spay next week

DIARY

Our other veterinarian returns later this afternoon from her conference in Florida. While I enjoy being alone and calling the shots on my own, it's good to have another doctor around to share the appointment load and provide feedback on diagnoses. At its best, veterinary medicine is a team effort. Two heads are often better than one when it comes to discussing cases and treatments.

One of our regular customers, a professional dog breeder, arrives today with two puppies. She's a responsible breeder because she carefully screens new owners to make sure her dogs will receive the proper care. We're giving them their first vaccinations and de-worming treatments. Both dogs, tiny Labrador retrievers, receive a thorough exam and their shots. Then one of our assistants brings in her newly adopted dog, Otis. A man formerly owned this dog but apparently didn't really want him, as the animal remained tied up outdoors day and night. Eventually Otis ended up at the local animal shelter, where our assistant works as a volunteer dog walker. We're seeing the dog today to treat his feet, which have suffered irritation from the ice and

THE PHONE CENTER AT THE REAR OF OUR OFFICE.

snow we've recently experienced. It's possible that Otis is afflicted with allergies, which along with his previous poor nutrition have combined to make his feet extra-sensitive. The snow, ice, and cold weather have caused them to bleed. We discuss putting Otis on a special diet designed to combat allergies, as well as applying petroleum jelly to his feet to help soften the pads.

Next I'm expecting Hamlet, who will have his bandage changed. Last Saturday, his owner walked in without an appointment and demanded to have his dog examined. He believed the dog had been caught in a coyote trap and, in the process of freeing himself, ripped off part of a toe. Looking at Hamlet's foot, I thought he might have a tumor on his toe, but I wasn't positive. His owner swore the toe had been normal that morning. I elected to wrap the toe for protection and put the dog on antibiotics to see if his foot might improve. If there is no improvement, we'll amputate the toe and send it to the lab for a biopsy. By lunchtime there's still no sign of Hamlet, so we chalk it up as yet another no-show.

This afternoon I'm scheduled to euthanize Eva, a 12-year-old exotic sled dog owned by a local merchant. She's one of the first dogs of this breed he's owned, and she has not being doing well of late. It's obvious she's lost a lot of weight, and her owner was forced to carry the dog into the office. I'm also told she has no control over her bladder and bowels and seems to be in considerable pain. I agree with his assessment and perform the task, knowing that she's finally found peace.

My colleague will arrive at four o'clock to take the evening shift. Since we stay open until 7:00 p.m. twice a week, on Tuesdays I work the evening hours and on Thursdays she does. Lynda the cat arrives for her pre-surgical exam. She's been in heat for the past month, and her owner is ready to have her spayed. It's our policy to schedule an exam with an owner and their pet before we perform surgery. We want to make sure the pet is otherwise healthy and has been kept up-to-date on vaccinations. Lynda's physical is normal, so we schedule her to be spayed on Tuesday.

My last appointment is Snowball, an American Eskimo dog with a funny ear. He's been scratching it for the last few months, but only today did his owners notice a swelling on his ear. I see what looks like an ear hematoma, which is a blood blister situated between the ear's cartilage flaps. He also has a bad case of fleas. It's likely the flea infestation caused him to scratch and shake his head so much that he ruptured some capillaries at the tip of his ear. I dispense some flea medicine and send them home. They decide to wait out the hematoma but, if it persists, they'll have it surgically lanced.

LESSONS/PROBLEMS

I'm much happier when I have colleagues around to share the workload. With some tumors, it can be difficult to tell whether they've occurred due to injury or if they're cancerous. Exams must be scheduled prior to surgery to make sure the patient is healthy enough to undergo the procedure.

INTUBATED CAT READY FOR HIS PROCEDURE.

Day 11 *JANUARY 19*

PREDICTIONS
- *Recheck Elsa, a grumpy diabetic cat*
- *Examine an elderly golden retriever that has been vomiting*

DIARY
Elsa is a grumpy 12-year-old longhaired cat I met during an emergency visit. She came in one Sunday because she wasn't eating and appeared lethargic. Upon running her blood work we discovered she was diabetic and had high kidney values. We kept her overnight on fluids and started insulin, but by the evening she wouldn't let us touch her. I sent her home the next day and her owners continued with fluids under the skin at home plus insulin injections. Today is her three-month checkup. We'll test her fructosamine

level, which gives us a more accurate reading than glucose to see how well regulated she is on her insulin. Whenever Elsa comes in, we follow a specific routine to cope with her extreme reaction. We carry her in her cage to the back room, where a towel is waiting to be draped over the cage door. Then we remove her from the carrier, hissing and spitting while wrapped in the towel. After drawing blood, we place her on the scale and then let her run back into her cage. This routine works well and our hands receive fewer scratches that way. Her test results will be back in a few days.

Following Elsa, Hamlet arrives unannounced. I'm glad his owner finally brought him in, but I wish they would adhere to our schedule. We make appointments to keep the day running smoothly and to make sure every patient gets the attention and time they deserve. When clients simply walk in, it throws off our routine and forces people to wait. Luckily they've arrived at the end of my appointment block, so I have time to do the exam. It's immediately apparent that Hamlet's owner should have come in when originally scheduled. I smelled a bad odor from the dog's foot the moment they entered the room. I'd recommended a bandage change two days after their original visit, and now nearly a week has passed. After pulling off the bandage I can see that it's a tumor, just as I suspected. Immediately we begin discussing amputation, but the owner tells me he doesn't have that kind of money. With that news I give him two options. He can either request financial aid from the shelter or a local nonprofit group that offers grants for this purpose, or else relinquish ownership to us at the hospital.

If he chooses the second option, I'll perform the surgery for the cost of materials only, but he'll sign over the right for us to find the dog a new home. The gentleman departs with additional antibiotics and promises to consider those two options.

After lunch it's time for Ralph, an elderly golden retriever who has been vomiting and losing weight for months. He looks emaciated to me, but his owners tell me he has more energy than ever. I think it's because the weight is off his arthritic joints, which allows him to move better. His owners are frustrated because Ralph had some blood work done a few months ago, but the results were inconclusive. I take a look at the previous doctor's notes and the test results, which are normal. After some pointed questioning I'm convinced Ralph is not vomiting at all but is instead regurgitating. Regurgitation is the spitting up of partially or undigested food from the esophagus, whereas vomiting is the forceful expulsion of bile or food from the stomach itself. Regurgitation occurs for reasons that are different from vomiting. I believe Ralph may be wasting away because very little food is reaching his stomach. His owners make it quite clear they don't wish to pay for any more diagnostics. They simply want to make him comfortable. I recommend a special food that is easily digested, but I want them to feed him in a standing position with the food rolled into tiny meatballs so it will slide down his esophagus more easily. I warn there could be more going on, such as cancer. If this treatment fails to yield improvement in his condition, they'll have to decide what to do next, either diagnostics or euthanasia. I am anxious to see how he performs.

LESSONS/PROBLEMS

Cats can be grumpy, so it's always a good idea to be prepared. If bandages are left on too long, they can turn smelly. The difference between vomiting and regurgitation isn't always obvious to a pet owner, and a good vet will ask the right questions to arrive at the proper diagnosis.

PREDICTIONS

- *Administer routine vaccinations*
- *Express anal glands for an unhappy patient*
- *Check out a lump on an elderly retriever*

DIARY

In the world of veterinary medicine, you never know what
Mondays will bring, especially if no doctor has been on duty
at the hospital through the weekend. Some people refuse to
visit a different clinic, even in an emergency, so they'll wait
until Monday to bring in their pet. Those clients can quickly
fill up an appointment book. However, such is not the case
today. Our morning schedule involves routine booster shots
plus one new patient. Everything goes smoothly and I'm
finished by 11 o'clock. The afternoon shouldn't be much
busier, so it will be one of those days where we do things
like wrap packs, copy papers, and clean up to stay active.

The excitement of the afternoon is Brady, an older Labrador
retriever mix being examined because she's scooting. We
are hardly Brandy's favorite people. In fact, I can't even get
close enough to her to apply a muzzle so she won't bite me.
Brandy was adopted from a shelter when she was about a
year old, and her early history is therefore unknown. Puppies
need to be socialized prior to four months of age—getting
them used to all sorts of people and different situations—or
else risk having them turn fearful. If a non-socialized animal

A SELECTION OF THE PRESCRIPTION PET FOODS WE SELL.

suffers a traumatic event or an unpleasant experience, it may hold a prejudice against that place or person for life. Veterinarians often fall into that category.

Behavioral problems are the top reason dogs end up in shelters every year, and the number two reason for cats. According to the Humane Society of the United States, it's estimated that from six million to eight million dogs and cats are surrendered to shelters each year, of which only about half are subsequently adopted. Some behavioral problems can be remedied if they're treated early. It's a veterinarian's job to help owners recognize and address these issues. Whenever I see a client with a new puppy or kitten, I'll mention some of the more common behavioral issues such as house breaking, jumping up, mouthing, chewing, litter box training, and basic obedience training. I'll also discuss being a good leader with dog owners, an important concept whether you have a puppy or an older dog. If an owner is not consistently a good leader, the dog may feel the need to assume that role, which will result in outward manifestations of fear and aggression. People can be good leaders by teaching their dogs that "nothing is for free." In other words, their dog has to ask for everything. Teaching a dog to sit does this. One reinforces this command by giving the dog nothing unless it sits, whether that means feeding, going for a walk, having a treat, or receiving affection. This concept can help dogs feel more comfortable and consequently less anxious or aggressive. I speak with Brandy's owner about trying this. Meanwhile, the client manages to get a muzzle over Brandy's nose without too much difficulty, and I call in one of my assistants to help me check the dog's anal glands. Brandy puts up a good fight, but I'm eventually able to express her glands. The fluid appears abnormal, so I put her on antibiotics and ask to see her again next week for another session. I want to make sure her glands stay empty and the infection is clearing up. I imagine Brandy will be even less happy to see me next time we meet.

Then we're visited by Sky, an older black Labrador whose owner is complaining about a lump on her body. I double-check Sky's chart and discover this very same lump was charted a few years ago and tested as a lipoma, which is a benign tumor comprised of fatty tissue. We're relieved to know it's not serious, and the client decides it's a good time to bring Sky's vaccinations up to date. She's also trying to get her dog to lose weight, knowing that a difference of even 10 pounds will make her a much more active and younger-looking pet.

LESSONS/PROBLEMS

Dogs adopted from animal shelters may not have received the proper amount of socialization, so they can be fearful and aggressive in certain situations. Without aspirating a bump in the skin, it's often difficult to judge its severity.

A DRAWER IN EXAM ROOM 2. AMONG THE CONTENTS ARE EYE STAINS. WE PLACE THESE STAINS IN EYES AND USE A BLUE LIGHT TO LOOK FOR CORNEAL SCRATCHES.

Day 13 *JANUARY 23*

PREDICTIONS

- *Perform a dental procedure on an older dog with bad teeth*
- *Examine an older cat that is not eating*
- *Treat a cat with a limp*

DIARY

I'm on call again and we have a nerve-racking dental treatment scheduled today. The client is a very nice woman who loves her dog very much. Her husband died a few years ago, and her animals are her life. The patient is a very old rescue dog of hers with a severe case of dental disease. After many months I've finally convinced her to allow me to perform the dental work on Fester. He has so many rotted teeth I know the benefits of doing this procedure far outweighs the risks. He'll feel much better once I'm finished. Because his liver values have been elevated lately, we'll run some blood work first to make sure they're within tolerable levels. It will take close to 30 minutes to receive the test results, so I decide to spay and neuter two cats that are awaiting surgery.

The feline procedures go well, so now it is Fester's turn in the theater. I decided to forgo intravenous anesthesia and use gas, which would allow the dog to wake up more quickly if we run into complications. Just the same, I insert an intravenous catheter to provide direct access to a vein throughout the procedure. I give Fester an injection of pain medication to help him relax, since I know I'll be pulling some teeth. The drug takes effect and we're able to mask him without incident. Once we begin the cleaning, it's immediately apparent we're doing the right thing. I'm forced to pull a dozen teeth because they're practically falling out of his mouth. We scale and polish the remainder and place a sealant on them. Fester's owner has promised to continue the weekly sealant treatments, which we hope will keep his mouth tartar-free. After he wakes, I call Fester's owner as promised. She's relieved the operation was a success, and we all let out a big sigh of relief as well. This turned out to be one of the most stressful dentals I've ever performed. I leave the office only after checking to see that Fester is able to stand on his own. On my way home I stop to pick up a soda, running into this morning's cat spay client at the checkout. I'm able to give her an update in person. This is one of those things about living in a small town that's both a blessing and a curse. No matter where you go, you're bound to run into a client.

Covering the evening shift is a breeze except for Teepee, a 12-year-old cat we're seeing because he's not eating. During the physical it seems there's a mass in his abdomen, but we start with some blood work since he's been losing weight. It doesn't take long to run the blood work and everything is fine, so I recommend that the owners allow me to take a radiograph to see if I can find a tumor. They'll consider it and get back to me.

My last appointment of the evening is a cat that was here a few weeks ago for its vaccinations. The owners don't know what happened, but the cat has been limping for the past 24 hours. We take his temperature and it's 104 degrees, which is fairly high for a cat. I also discover that one of his toes is swollen. I'm thinking that he got into a fight with another cat. I send him home on antibiotics and specific instructions for his owner to soak the foot. We provide a rabies booster because it's been more than thirty days since his last vaccination and the bite wound is of unknown origin. We also place him in home quarantine, and I recommend that he return in three months to be tested for feline leukemia and feline AIDS, since we don't know what diseases the animal that bit him may have been carrying.

LESSONS/PROBLEMS

If owners are fearful and emotional about leaving their pets with us for treatment, staff members may become unnecessarily tense. In a small town, everyone seems to recognize the vet. Any cat that has been in a fight needs to receive a rabies booster.

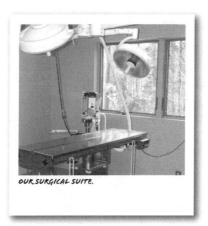
OUR SURGICAL SUITE.

Day 14 JANUARY 25

PREDICTIONS
- *Issue a health certificate*
- *See a new patient that is overweight*
- *Treat a dog for vomiting*

DIARY
My nine o'clock appointment is a 10-year-old cat. Bennie's owner recently passed away, and a family member is taking him home to California. Since Bennie will be transported via commercial aircraft, he will need a health certificate prior to boarding. Veterinarians who issue health certificates for domestic travel need no special licensing. However, accreditation is necessary to be permitted to write international health certificates. Veterinarians must

be accredited in the state in which they practice. Last September I attended a seminar in Augusta, our state capital. Part of the training involved a meeting with U.S. Department of Agriculture officials. We toured the state's laboratory and took a refresher course on filling out various forms. There was also a class on USDA shipping regulations and the organization's policies and procedures. Upon completing the course, I was licensed to issue international health forms. Since we're not far from Canada and we also have clients with summer homes in Mexico, we do a fair amount of international business. These certificates include a description of the pet as well as a detailed history of their vaccinations, including serial numbers and expiration dates. For international travel, the client takes the completed health certificate to the USDA veterinarian in Augusta for a counter-signature. An approved certificate is valid for 30 days.

From Bennie I turn to Benji. He's a sweet dog but seriously needs to lose weight. Overweight pets are a growing epidemic in this country. Those extra pounds have been shown to reduce a dog or cat's life by two years and contribute to heart disease, joint problems, and diabetes. While there can be medical reasons for weight gain, most of the time it's the result of a bad diet, overfeeding, lack of exercise, or all three. That's certainly the case for Benji. During the exam I warn Benji's owner of the risks, strongly urging her to help him drop some weight, but she isn't terribly receptive.

Next up is Max, a three-year-old Portuguese water dog

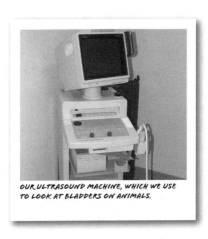

OUR ULTRASOUND MACHINE, WHICH WE USE TO LOOK AT BLADDERS ON ANIMALS.

that began vomiting last night. His owner isn't sure if he got into anything but finds that unlikely since she restricts what he eats. He roams a fenced-in yard and does not receive table scraps. Max appears depressed, and his abdomen hurts so much when I palpate it that he actually screams. I recommend keeping him overnight and running some diagnostic tests to see what's going on. He's my last appointment of the morning, so I round up the troops and we draw some blood to run a full blood panel on him. We also warm up the x-ray machine for some radiographs. Twenty minutes later I'm in possession of both results. Max's blood work shows an Amylase that is not reading, and his radiographs do not reveal much more data. I suspect pancreatitis, but I still can't rule out a foreign body. After speaking with Max's owner, we decide to admit him and administer IV fluids to treat his dehydration. She also agrees to a test called canine-specific lipase. We'll use the results of this process to test my diagnosis of pancreatitis. Unfortunately the results must come from an outside lab, so it will be a day or two before we hear back. By then I expect he'll have improved thanks to the treatments we're starting today.

LESSONS/PROBLEMS

A health certificate is necessary to fly a pet overseas or between countries, and a veterinarian needs to be accredited to make it valid. Many dogs are overweight, and owners must take responsibility for many of the causes of that condition. When a dog is vomiting, that can mean many things.

PREDICTIONS

- *Diagnose a foreign body in Max's intestines*
- *See many routine appointments*

DIARY

Today I have a number of routine appointments scheduled, such as treating ear infections and a bladder infection plus giving out vaccinations, but the day truly revolves around Max. He continued to vomit throughout the night, which means it's time for more tests. Our options include a barium series, ultrasound, or basic exploratory surgery. Each one of these options has its positive and negative sides. The barium series is time-consuming to perform. The dog is given barium—a contrast material—and then we take a series of radiographs over a four-hour period. The contrast material helps highlight foreign bodies that may not show up on a standard radiograph, such as cloth or other non-metallic material. Sometimes the administration of the barium itself is all you need, as it coats the stomach and the intestines and has a tendency to halt the vomiting on its own. An ultrasound is the least time-consuming and minimally invasive option. While the ultrasound process may not necessarily highlight a foreign body, it allows us to detect suspicious areas plus it does a good job of depicting the pancreas. The final option involves exploratory surgery, by far the most invasive option but also the one that offers the greatest level of diagnostics. But unless you find something via radiography such as a rock or a ball, you'll often go into surgery strictly on circumstantial evidence. Because of that, it's quite possible you'll find nothing at all when you operate.

We decide to do a barium series on Max. After administering around 200 milliliters of barium we take an immediate radiograph. We then capture radiograph images every 15 minutes for a full hour. At this point the dog's stomach should have passed all the material to the intestines, but I see that Max has retained most of it. This makes me think something is preventing the stomach from emptying entirely, although the pain medication we gave him earlier can also slow down the GI tract. At the two-hour mark, Max's stomach is still full of barium and I see something in the small intestines that could be a band of material. I call his owner to see if she knows of anything he might have eaten. She recalls the dog pulled some knee-high stockings out of the trash a few days ago, but the incident didn't concern her because she assumed all he did was shred them with his teeth and claws. We decide to wait until the four-hour radiograph can be viewed, at which point it's clear that surgery is required.

At four o'clock, my colleague begins the operation while I finish up my appointments. She made three separate incisions in Max's intestines and pulled out three knee-high stockings by the time I arrive in surgery to assist her. We're worried because there are several spots in his intestines that don't look healthy. She proceeds onto the stomach

ERIN RUNS SOME BLOOD WORK.

and withdraws yet another stocking. By manipulating his stomach, however, Max has vomited up quite a large volume of barium. It comes pouring out of his mouth. Fortunately we had an endotracheal tube in place, and its inflated cuff should have prevented any of the liquid from entering his lungs. Sadly, the area of his intestines where the stockings were lodged has turned black, which means the damage is extensive. This section of his intestines will need to be removed. After snipping off 26 linear inches and their subsequent resection, we're fairly nervous. There remain several other questionable areas along the intestines, but it doesn't seem wise to remove any more at this time. When animals swallow things like strings, underwear, or stockings, such objects can cut through the intestines as the body tries to move them down the GI tract. This sawing motion damages the intestines and may lead to the leakage of intestinal fluid into the abdomen, resulting in peritonitis. Max's situation will be touch-and-go for the next two weeks. After closing Max up and making him comfortable in recovery, I call Max's owner and tell her what we found. My colleague will come back at nine o'clock to check on him, and I'll show up just before midnight to give him his medication.

LESSONS/PROBLEMS

Foreign bodies are not always evident under standard radiography. There are several options available to the vet that can help rule out foreign bodies, some more invasive than others. Leaking at the surgical site, with the potential to turn into peritonitis, can take up to two weeks to become evident.

OUR DOG RUN FOR LARGER CANINES.

Day 16 *JANUARY 27*

PREDICTIONS
- *Examine a cat for conjunctivitis*
- *See a golden retriever with a sore leg*
- *Continue monitoring Max and his intestinal problems*

DIARY
Max is still in the hospital, so he's my first stop when I show up today. We've decided to begin feeding him, but he hasn't shown any interest in food so far. His vital signs are all normal and he goes outside to urinate. We continue to administer antibiotics and fluids. His owner will come in later for a visit.

My first scheduled appointment is Charlie. He was originally a stray and then given to the hospital by a client who owns 20 other cats. The daughter of one of our assistants adopted him. He's a very nice cat but hates having his face touched. For the past week he's suffered from a runny eye, which has not improved with medication. He also has a history of gingivitis and diarrhea. I recommended testing him for feline bartonella to see if it can be blamed for his chronic aliments. This is a bacterium that cats can acquire after being exposed to infected fleas. It's often found in nail beds and passed on to humans through scratch wounds, thereby potentially causing cat-scratch disease. It's yet another of the many diseases that can move from pets to humans.

Next I see Bo, a 10-year-old golden retriever who hurt his leg while running after some ducks. Bo hates his visits to the vet, so we're forced to muzzle him. I examine his legs, and it feels like he may have ruptured a cruciate ligament. I decide to place him on an anti-inflammatory, and we schedule a series of radiographs for next Tuesday. We'll have more people around then to handle him, plus there will be additional time to sedate him. Without sedation, Bo will definitely not tolerate the radiography.

My next visitor is an emergency patient. Jack, a 15-year-old Lab, was in not too long ago because his back legs are getting weaker. He's here today because his owners think he might have a dislocated shoulder. They tell me Jack went out this morning to urinate and they heard him cry out. Since then he's been unable to put any weight on his front leg. After a brief exam I recommend a radiograph so we can

A CAT RECEIVING A LION CUT TO SHAVE OFF HIS MATS.

see what's going on. The x-rays show that Jack has a broken humerus, which is the bone between his shoulder and elbow. Jack's owners now have a tough decision to make. It's certainly possible that an orthopedist can repair the fracture, but the dog's recovery time will be a long and painful one due to his arthritis and the neurological deficiencies already present in his hind legs. His owners elect to euthanize him.

At ten o'clock, Max's owner comes in for a visit. The dog is clearly happy to see her, and she manages to feed him a bit. Then she takes him for a short walk and leaves behind her sweatshirt so he'll have a familiar scent around him. I see a few more patients for vaccinations, and then I draw some blood for a thyroid profile on a yellow Lab. This evening I'm going to a concert in Portland. On my way home, I'll stop in to check on Max. At 1:00 a.m. I return to the hospital to change out Max's fluids and take him for a walk. He's still not showing any interest in food.

LESSONS/PROBLEMS

There are many zoonotic diseases, which are afflictions that can be easily transmitted from animals to humans. For pet owners, euthanasia can be the most difficult decision they make.

Day 17 *JANUARY 28*

PREDICTIONS
- *Neuter cats at the animal shelter*
- *Start Max on a new antibiotic*

DIARY

I return to the hospital at 7:30 a.m. and check on Max.
His temperature is slightly elevated and he continues to
resist eating. I'm worried about infection as I give him his
morning dose of antibiotics. Then it's time to prepare for
the neuter clinic. I gather up all the supplies we'll need
including Epinephrine, Atropine, and so on, in case there's
an emergency. Our local animal shelter asks veterinarians in
the area to donate their time and neuter male cats that live
in our county. Our other vet volunteered last month, and
this month it's my turn. This is my first time participating in
one of these events. I'm pleased that one of my assistants
has volunteered to help me today. The facilities are quite
limited, as we're asked to perform the surgery on a table in
an upstairs office. Each doctor brings his or her own supplies
including sanitary scrub, clippers, and anesthetic. Because
of the limited facilities, we're doing only male cats. The
owners are not required to pay for this service, but they're
responsible for bringing their cat to the shelter and picking it
up after the surgery is over.

We have 15 cats today and line them up in groups of
five. Some of these cats look like they've never seen a

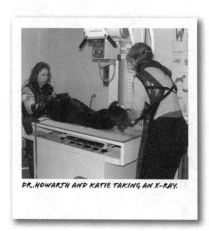
DR. HOWARTH AND KATIE TAKING AN X-RAY.

veterinarian, and I'm afraid that's very likely the case. We use an IV anesthetic—Telazol—to sedate the cats, and then we clip and scrub them. It's truly assembly-line surgery. First we weigh and sedate each group, and then I start at one end of the line to neuter them. Since Telazol takes only a few minutes to work, the first cat in the group is asleep by the time we get to the end of the pack. Following the procedure we monitor them closely until they wake up. Telazol is a good short-term anesthetic used most often in cats, but dogs can take it as well. It's nice because you have the flexibility to administer it intravenously or as an IM anesthetic, which means in the muscle. This latter technique is quite helpful whenever you have an aggressive dog or cat, since all you have to do is aim and shoot. Once injected, the animal usually stays sedated for 30 minutes before beginning to wake up. It can also be used in conjunction with gas anesthesia to lengthen the time needed to complete a more complicated procedure.

After the clinic, I return to the hospital. My colleague checked on Max while I was gone, and I take a moment to call up his owner. She arrives shortly for a visit, but she's able to get him to eat only a small amount of food. After she leaves, I decide to run some blood work on him to check his white blood cell count (WBC) and electrolytes. Unfortunately, his WBC is elevated, which can indicate peritonitis. His potassium level is low, so I decide to supplement his fluids with potassium. I start him on an intravenous combination of Metronidazole and Baytril, which is on top of the other antibiotic—Cefazolin—he's getting every eight hours. It's our goal to wipe out all the bacteria that might be lingering in his abdomen. To give Max his medication, I take him out of his cage and start the Metronidazole on an IV drip. We're lucky to have one 500mg pouch in stock. Max is a good boy and remains still while the antibiotic runs through the tubing. After it's finished I take him outside so he'll use the bathroom, and he then walks quietly back into his cage for the night. I tell him I'll be back later to see how he's doing. I hope he's all right because I'm very worried he might not make it.

I return to check on Max at 11 o'clock. It's an especially dark night and I hear coyotes yipping in the woods behind the hospital. That's an eerie sound! Max still won't eat anything, but he does come outside with me and seems a little perkier. Tomorrow I may send him home to see how that works. His owner will like that. He's a very special dog.

LESSONS/PROBLEMS

Max doesn't seem to be getting any better, despite all the antibiotics he's had and whatever other efforts we've made. The sort of community service I did today—neutering all those cats—is a satisfying part of my job because I'm able to helping people accomplish something they couldn't otherwise afford.

PREDICTIONS

- *See if Max can go home to recuperate*
- *Remove sutures from a previous surgery*
- *Check out a rescued basset hound with a sore back*

DIARY

The first thing I do upon arriving at the office is check on Max. He still is not eating much. I call his owner to see if she's willing to look after him at home, and she eagerly accepts the assignment. I write out a prescription for Prilosec and send him home on all three antibiotics. The Prilosec should ease the inflammation and irritation in his esophagus that was caused by the vomiting he did during surgery. I'm hopeful a less sore throat will make him want to eat more. I recommend to his owner that she take him for a long walk to get his bowels moving, and then try to get him to eat. We're not out of the woods just yet.

It looks like it will be slow today. I have only five appointments this morning, and one of them is an anal gland recheck. All my vaccinations go smoothly, and the most interesting case of the day is the recheck from last week. Brandy's anal glands are impacted and need to be expressed. The discharge looks much better than on her last visit. We're still forced to muzzle her, but the device slipped on a bit more easily this time. After lunch, I have only four more appointments. One of those involves removing some sutures. Two weeks ago, Austin was neutered and his rear dewclaws were removed. Dewclaws are usually removed when a puppy is less than five days old, but some breeders don't have that done. We prefer to leave them in place unless they're causing a problem or as long as a true joint is present. In Austin's case there was no actual joint there, and he kept catching them on things. Also, his owner was having trouble cutting the nail. All of these signs indicate removal. Austin is a well-behaved dog, and he lies nice and still on his back so I can remove the sutures. The incision looks good but it's still a bit red. I pull out the sutures, recommending that the owner keep his conical collar in place for a few more days so he can't lick the incision and cause an infection.

After Austin, Cleo comes in. She was recently rescued from somewhere down south, and her owner noticed she seems especially uncomfortable. She's very skinny and has a lot of debris in her ears, which is not unusual for a basset hound. During her physical she reacts noticeably when I touch her back, so I recommend radiography. Her owner agrees to the procedure but asks us to keep the dog overnight, since she has to go to work. We take the radiographs and observe that Cleo has two disks spaces in her back that appear unusually narrow. This indicates a collapsed or herniated disk called inter-vertebral disc disease, or IVDD. Immediate treatment includes Prednisone—a steroid to reduce inflammation—plus muscle relaxants and cage rest for four to six weeks. Cage rest is important because, as she begins to feel better, I don't want her moving around too much and re-injuring herself. We start Cleo immediately on Prednisone and set her up for the night.

Every mammal has a vertebral column, or spine. The bones of the vertebrae surround the spinal cord for protection. In between each vertebra is a disc, which prevents bone-on-bone contact. In its optimal state this disc is gelatinous. But in older animals and those with a genetic predisposition—dachshunds are one such example—this gelatin can harden and calcify. When a dog or cat twists suddenly or the wrong way, this now-calcified disc may intrude into the space that surrounds the spinal column or else rupture into that space. When this occurs, the spinal cord swells in response. Since it's encased in bone, it can only swell so much. This puts pressure on the outside tracts of the spinal cord, which then causes pain. In some severe situations it may even result in paralysis. Observable clinical signs vary based on the location of the disc protrusion. The cervical spine is much wider than in the thoracic and lumbar areas, and the bigger the spinal canal the more swelling that can occur. This is why dogs with a slipped disc in their neck will experience pain, but a similar situation in the lumbar spine can cause paralysis. If pain is present, steroids will often alleviate the condition, but paralysis requires surgery. We're fortunate that Cleo is only experiencing pain, so the medications we're giving should make her better.

LESSONS/PROBLEMS

Sometimes animals do better at home when recovering from surgery. Dogs should have their dewclaws removed if they're causing problems, or if it proves difficult to cut the nail. Herniated spinal disks can be very painful, although the seriousness of the condition depends greatly on the location.

OUR WAITING ROOM.

Day 19 *JANUARY 30*

PREDICTIONS

- *Check out Beau's sore leg by employing radiography*
- *Radiograph a cat with chronic urinary issues*
- *See two new patients*

DIARY

We have a very full schedule today, but most of our more serious patients are coming in for radiographs. Beau is the first one to arrive this morning. He's the large golden retriever with a sore leg we saw on Saturday. We elect to do him first because he doesn't like coming here, and we need to sedate him for the radiographs. After a struggle, we finally manage to get a muzzle on him and administer the anesthesia, in this case a mixture of Ketamine and Valium.

This is a very good combination to use when your procedure is expected to be brief. He should be up and around in 30 minutes or so, which is a positive aspect of this blend. The downside is that we'll have to move fast. We manage to get some very good pictures and my suspicions are correct; he has a ruptured cruciate ligament. His owner agrees to schedule him for surgery next week.

Next up is Barak, an older cat who has been suffering urinary problems for quite some time. Recently he's been urinating blood throughout the house. A short while ago we performed a urinalysis and detected an infection, so he's already on antibiotics. Today we need to find out why his infections keep returning. Three questions come immediately to mind. Does he have bladder stones? Is he on the proper antibiotic? Has that antibiotic been given a long enough time to do its job? First we radiograph him, which shows no visible bladder stones. Then we collect a sterile urine sample to be cultured. This will confirm whether Barak has an infection and, if so, which antibiotic is the best choice for treatment.

The cat we're expecting to neuter is a no-show. That's hardly surprising, since the phone number the folks left when they scheduled the appointment turns out to be disconnected. However, our cat to be spayed is here. I perform the procedure and administer a booster to her feline AIDS vaccination. Her vaccination schedule is now complete.

While I'm home for lunch I'm paged by a client of one of

the other hospitals in the area. She has a question about her cat, which is a diabetic. She is worried because the cat seems a bit off to her. She rejects my suggestion to bring her animal over to our clinic, as she plans to speak with her regular vet when their office opens at two o'clock. Just the same, she's wondering what to give her cat if it's suffering from low blood sugar. I explain that a teaspoon of Karo syrup would do the trick, if that were her concern. Still at lunch, Max's owner calls to tell me he had a bowel movement, which is good, and she's managed to get him to eat a bit, which is excellent. I offer her additional words of encouragement before heading back to the office. Our collection of afternoon appointments include Candy, Abi, Dixie, Tinkerbell, Emmma, and Zoë. These last two are new patients, while the rest are coming in for vaccination boosters.

New patients are always good for a practice, and especially so in our area. Unlike where I lived in New Jersey, with developers constantly turning farmland into new housing tracts, this part of Maine is fairly stable as far as growth is concerned. We acquire new clients for a variety of reasons, including people who move into the area from elsewhere. Sometimes the person doesn't like their existing veterinarian or they're not happy about the hours the clinic keeps. We also have quite a few cottages in the region, and many seasonal visitors bring their pets along for the summer. These are vacationers as well as people who own a second home up here. Some clients stick with us, and some we never see again. One of the best measures of a healthy practice is by counting the number of new clients you retain. The software we use in our office helps keep track of that.

LESSONS/PROBLEMS

Sometimes animals recover better at home. A sterile urine collection and subsequent culture is often needed to determine the best antibiotics for an infection, or if there's an infection at all. Clients who have out-of-service phone numbers are not likely to show up for their appointments.

PREDICTIONS

- *Attend a continuing education seminar*

DIARY

I'm up at five o'clock this morning to reach my seminar in Portland by eight. Today I'm attending a continuing education (CE) class on anesthesia, which is perfect timing since I've promised to discuss this very same topic with our technicians at the clinic. Our state's veterinary medical association is sponsoring this particular CE, so it's a smaller gathering than some of the other CEs I often attend. I've only lived in Maine for eight months, and I'm not well acquainted with many of the vets in the state just yet. Because I'd worked in the New Jersey area for nine years, I knew quite a few of the local veterinarians. Many of these CEs are as much social events as they are educational.

Strangely enough, I do run into a former New Jersey veterinarian. During the time I was at an animal hospital in Mount Holly, this doctor worked at the clinic in Mount Laurel run by the same people who owned ours. He also had his own mobile veterinary clinic and worked three days a week out of Larchmont. He's a terrific surgeon, and I called on him whenever we ran into more complicated cases. In fact, there was a time he performed bladder surgery on one of my patients while I went to Larchmont and covered his appointments. He tells me how much he loves Maine. He

OUR X-RAY ROOM. THE CHART WE USE FOR THE SETTINGS, AND THE LEAD GOWNS WE WEAR WHILE TAKING RADIOGRAPHS.

opened a house-call practice in the area and also does relief work one or two days a week. We exchange phone numbers and agree to meet over dinner some time soon.

The first section of today's CE is on acid-base disturbances and fluid replacement. I find the lecture rather boring, but there are a few interesting tidbits worth noting. The presenter is a graduate of the American College of Veterinary Internal Medicine. She begins by discussing basic theory and then presents multiple cases to show us the practical side to what we're learning. I have a hard time staying awake, but they have some muffins and orange juice on the refreshment table that helps perk me up.

My phone starts to vibrate during the lecture, and I check the number to see that someone from my office is calling. During the break I ring them back. Max's owner reports that his most recent bowel movement was diarrhea, and then he vomited. This is hardly normal under the circumstances, and I'm very concerned. Coincidentally, our other doctor left work with vomiting and diarrhea herself, so there's no vet on hand at the moment. At my insistence, one of our assistants checks with Max's owner. When I speak with our assistant again, I'm told the dog is resting comfortably. Max's owner was instructed to call us again if he continues to vomit. He's already scheduled for a recheck appointment tomorrow.

After the morning session we break for lunch, which includes a speech by the president-elect of the American Veterinary Medical Association plus a few words from the new president of our state association. A woman veterinarian from Afghanistan is the next speaker on the agenda, and what she has to say I find very interesting. The state veterinarian discusses Maine's recent increase in rabies cases, and then our lunch meeting is adjourned.

Anesthesia monitoring is the topic of the afternoon session, and the speaker is a world-renowned anesthesiologist from Ohio. He explains the different kinds of anesthesia in use as well as the best combinations of drugs that can be employed to achieve an anesthetic state. He completes his two-hour session by discussing the importance of monitoring the anesthetized patient and which equipment does the best job. I find this portion fascinating, especially since we just purchased the two machines he claims are tops.

LESSONS/PROBLEMS

Veterinarians who wish to retain their state licensure are often required to take continuing education courses. These lectures can be a great source of information as well as serving to remind you of things you'd forgotten since attending vet school.

PREDICTIONS

- *Run diagnostics on a young kitten with a fever*
- *Recheck an ear that is infected*

DIARY

Max is my first appointment of the day. The single instance of vomiting and diarrhea he suffered yesterday has not recurred, but he's still not eating very much. His incision looks good, his abdomen is not painful to the touch, and his temperature is normal. We draw blood to recheck his white blood cell count, and I send him home with renewed hope. It's been six days since his surgery, and thankfully he appears to be on the mend.

I have two rabies-only vaccinations before seeing Ozzie, a four-month-old kitten that has not been eating well for several days. His temperature is high and he's lost some weight since his last visit. Other than his elevated temperature and thin body condition, I find nothing remarkable on his exam. We decide to test him for feline leukemia and feline AIDS as well as doing some other blood work. However, we can't get much blood out of him since he's so tiny. The FELV/FIV test comes back negative, and we manage just enough blood to run a PCV. Those test results indicate anemia, and a blood smear we do show a decreased white blood cell count. Ozzie is a shelter cat, so I warn his owner about the various diseases that can affect young cats, such as FIP and toxoplasmosis. We decide to treat him with antibiotics, and I'll recheck him in a few days if his condition hasn't improved.

My last appointment of the morning is Doyle, a cat owned by a very kind man who has a knack for adopting the sickest animals from the local shelter. Doyle is quite ill. He has a temperature of 104, has lost a fair amount of weight, and is not eating. The gentleman has seen this situation before, unfortunately. Over the past three months he's lost two other cats to the exact same symptoms. With those cats we ran a battery of tests and came to the conclusion they had FIP. This is a highly infectious feline disease that presents itself in two forms, wet and dry. Both versions cause a high fever, loss of appetite and weight, plus in the wet form fluid builds up in the abdomen. The disease is hard to diagnose without a biopsy, but it's always fatal. I see that Doyle's abdomen is beginning to fill with fluid, so I take a sample. It's yellow, just like with the others. His owner already feared what we would find, and he knows what will happen next. Doyle is still eating a little, so we send him home for the weekend so his owner can spend a little more time with him.

I return from lunch at 1:30 P.M. to perform a euthanasia. Rudy is a 17-year-old beagle that has not been doing well for the past few months. His gums are pale and he has limited awareness of his surroundings. I give him a mild sedative to help him relax before the final injections are administered. Euthanasia is one of the hardest parts of being a veterinarian. It's one aspect of the practice I took to poorly. Right after graduation from vet school, I began having nightmares about the animals I'd euthanized. I believe part of the reason for those nightmares involved my inability to control which animals I would and would not euthanize. We were required to perform this procedure whenever an owner requested it. As time went on and I became more confident with my skills as a veterinarian, I learned how to say no and was given the power to refuse those who wanted euthanasia simply for convenience. Today is different, as it's an opportunity to give an animal peace and relief from suffering.

After Rudy I perform several more routine exams. Then it's time for Mr. Peaches, one of my favorite patients. He's a very sweet dog who lets me do anything to him without complaining. Today we're checking his ear, which has been infected for several months. I've already done ear cytology and a culture, but the ear has refused to clear up. His owners even placed him on a special diet, but that has had no effect. We discuss allergy testing and an endoscopy that will look down his ear canal, but the best recommendation I can make involves a trip to the surgeon. Mr. Peaches has difficulty taking medication, and every night blood from his ear sprays on the walls when he shakes his head. We've also had him on two different antibiotics, both separately and together. It's time for a surgical evaluation to remove the inner workings of that ear. A total ear ablation is the only cure for chronic ear infections, and his owners leave the office with a promise to strongly consider this option.

LESSONS/PROBLEMS

Animals adopted from a shelter have a much higher potential to be ill. These pets are exposed to many different infectious diseases and they often lack adequate vaccinations. With chronic ear infections, sometimes the only way to cure them is by removing the inner workings.

PREDICTIONS
- *Examine a cat with urinary problems*
- *Treat a dog with a bad cough*
- *Keep an appointment with a very ill dog*

DIARY

My first appointment this morning is Spook, a cat we saw a few weeks ago for a radiograph and a urine culture. She's suffering from recurring bladder infections and her owner wants to know why. I see from her pictures that urinary calculi are not indicated, which is good news. We run into a small problem, however, while attempting to obtain a sterile urine sample. Every time we place the cat on her back, she urinates. The stream contains blood and her perineal region is red and raw. We collect what we can and run a urinalysis. I call her owner to explain that since Spook is overweight, she can't reach around and clean herself properly. Because she can't keep herself clean, her owner will have to do that for her. I also discuss our lack of success in collecting a sterile sample. We decide to send her home on antibiotics and will try again in two weeks, when we hope her bladder will be less spastic.

It's unusual to treat two cats with the same condition on the same day. Barak's urine culture results have come in. We see no evidence of infection, so he apparently has inflammatory cystitis. This can be a result of feline lower urinary tract disease, a common condition in cats and one that's potentially fatal in males. The exact cause isn't known, but genetics can be a factor. The best treatment involves reducing the number of flare-ups a cat suffers. This can be accomplished through a special diet and by taking such additives as Cosequin or glucosamine. Reducing stress helps, as does drinking plenty of water. I give the news to Barak's owners, who will try Cosequin and a change in diet.

Then I see a new cat that spends most of its time hiding under the bed. Her vaccination schedule has not been kept up to date, but her owner insists she hasn't been outside in a long time. Her physical is normal but her temperature is somewhat elevated. I tell her owner that although I don't see anything obvious today, these things have a way of revealing themselves over time. I recommend she watch very closely for other clues as to what might be going on. It sure would be great if my patients could talk.

Gidget is next. She came home from the kennel last week and is now coughing. She's a young, healthy dog with no clinical signs other than the cough, which occurs whenever she gets excited or lies down. I palpate her trachea, which sets off a coughing frenzy. My diagnosis is kennel cough, more technically known as bordatella. This is a fairly common disease in dogs, mainly because it's airborne. It's often seen in dogs that have been in close quarters, such as in a boarding facility or at a dog show. Thankfully it's usually self-limiting and fairly easy to treat. I start Gidget on antibiotics and a cough medicine to ease her symptoms, especially at night. She should be feeling much better in just a few days.

My final appointment before lunch is a cat that belongs to one of our receptionist's friends. Apparently Whitebeard was in a fight with another cat and now has a bite wound on his head. I shave the area and remove a fair amount of pus. The cat gets a rabies booster and will be started on antibiotics. He's also ordered into a 45-day quarantine.

Up first this afternoon is a cat with an upper respiratory infection. That's an easy thing to treat, but my next patient is very ill. The dog's owner reports that the animal has appeared much more tired than usual, and he's had difficulty standing up and lying down. I do a physical and don't like the color of his gums, so I draw blood and send him home. Before they leave, I tell his owner that I'm not sure what's going on with Kay, but the blood test will help give us more information. I'm especially interested to see the red blood cell count.

After Kay I have seven more patients. These are all routine vaccinations except for the last one. Dog is a huge Saint Bernard with a knack for getting into things he shouldn't. We've pulled porcupine quills from his skin something like five times now, which has to be a record. This time he's being seen for vomiting and diarrhea. His owners can't explain the cause, but I'm pleased to report that his physical comes up normal. I send him home on some Metronidazole and a recommendation for a bland diet. They'll let me know if that doesn't do the trick.

Kay's blood work is finished. My fears are confirmed. He has a very low red blood cell count. I call his owner to report that Kay has a disease called autoimmune hemolytic anemia, but so far I'm not sure of the cause. Because Kay's numbers are at a very critical level, he should be taken immediately to the round-the-clock emergency clinic in Portland for a blood transfusion. Down there they'll do radiographs, tick serology, and possible an ultrasound to find out if Kay has underlying cancer or some other incitement for the AIHA. They'll also start him on some immunosuppressive medications and hospitalize him over the weekend.

LESSONS/PROBLEMS
Overweight cats oftentimes have difficulty in grooming themselves, which can lead to a urinary tract infection. Vaccinating against bordatella should be done whenever a dog is headed for a kennel or anywhere else canines are likely to gather. Some dogs develop severe anemia and subsequently require a blood transfusion.

PREDICTIONS

- *Examine a cat from a home with 12 other felines*
- *Draw blood work for a dog on seizure medication*
- *Treat an itchy dog*

DIARY

This morning I find out that Max came in to see our other doctor over the weekend because he started vomiting again. His exam showed an elevated temperature and he was complaining of abdominal pain. Options were discussed with his owner, including additional surgery to remove more of his damaged intestines. They decided the best thing for Max was to euthanize him. Also on my desk this morning is a report from this weekend's emergency doctor. It's in reference to the cat I saw on Friday that was always hiding under the bed. Her condition had deteriorated and she was having trouble opening her mouth. The doctor-on-call found an abscess. They kept her overnight and today will surgically insert a drain.

My first appointment is another one of the Labrador puppies I've been seeing over the past two weeks. This is the last of the litter to find a home. The owner tells me the new owners happen to run a local motorcycle shop. The breeder is excited because she'll be able to see the dog grow up, since these two families have a number of friends in common.

TODAY'S SURGERY PATIENTS.

JoJo is next, a cat whose owners have 13 in all. One of the older cats of the bunch, Jojo is due for her annual wellness exam and vaccinations. I happen to notice evidence of flea dirt in her fur. Whenever you see flea dirt and live fleas on a cat, that's likely to represent only about five percent of the total flea population. All the rest of the fleas are in the house. With 13 cats, solving this infestation will be quite a challenge. Each cat will require individual flea prevention efforts and the house will probably have to be fumigated.

One of our assistants arrives with her dog, Otis. He's here to have sutures removed following his recent eye surgery. Otis has a condition called entropion, which causes his lower eyelid to roll inward. Our other doctor did this work on him a few weeks ago, but the difficulty continued so he returned to have a tiny bit more of the eyelid sliced off. This extra surgery did the trick, so today we can snip out his sutures.

Then Katie returns because she's still having trouble with her eye. This is the third recheck we're doing on this dog as we monitor a scratch on her cornea. It's taking a long time to heal. I suggested taking her to an ophthalmologist for an evaluation, but her owners don't wish to make the two-hour trip to this doctor's New Hampshire office. They'll simply have to be patient, since older dogs heal slowly. It may take several more months before the scratch clears up.

My first two appointments this afternoon both involve seizures. Swiffer is a three-year-old pointer that has been having seizures for more than two years. She's received an evaluation by a neurologist and has been doing fairly well on two different seizure medications. Today we draw blood to establish a monitoring level on her seizure meds and to check her liver function. We're not doing an exam today, as she has an appointment with the neurologist next week. I simply draw the blood, run the tests, and then fax them to her specialist in Portland. Then I see a three-year-old beagle that had her first seizure two days ago. Her physical is normal but we draw blood to test her for underlying abnormalities. Her blood work comes back normal, which is good. The next step is to monitor her closely. If her seizures become more frequent or violent, we'll start her on medication.

Last up this afternoon is Nathan, a two-year-old Maltese that has been scratching for the past two weeks. His skin is quite pink, but I detect no wounds on his fur from the chewing. We talk about the possibility of sarcoptic mange and allergies. In Maine, sarcoptic mange is fairly common. When I first moved here, I had no idea how common this mite was and consequently often missed diagnosing it. Now it's one of the first things I consider when coming across an itchy dog. Foxes are a prime source, and most dogs in this area aren't confined to a fenced-in yard, so transmission between the two populations is fairly common. Treatment calls for Ivomectin in two or three injections. Applying Ivomectin in this manner is an off-label use, which means it's not an FDA-approved treatment. However, we have very few effective options. It may take more than two weeks for the dog's owner to see a reduction in the itching, but once the medicine takes hold it makes all the difference in the world. Nathan's owner elects not to go for the Ivomectin, so instead we treat him for allergies. If this regimen fails to solve the itch problem, we may try a special food trial or some similar allergy testing—and then there's always the Ivomectin.

LESSONS/PROBLEMS

People who own a lot of cats, especially cats that spend time outdoors, are likely to see fleas. Many different things can cause seizures. Sarcoptic mange is a common parasitic disease in Maine, although it can often be difficult to distinguish from allergies.

A KITTY WAKING FROM ANESTHESIA.

Day 24 *FEBRUARY 6*

PREDICTIONS
- *Recheck a feverish kitten*
- *Stay busy in the afternoon with wellness exams*
- *Handle emergency calls whenever they may come in*

DIARY
It's another on-call Tuesday for me. This morning I have
two spays, a cat neuter, and a dental. Ozzie is also planning
a return visit. His owner tells me he hasn't improved since
the last time we saw him, so today we'll try to extract
more blood for the toxoplasmosis titer, which is a measure
of the level of antibodies present in the bloodstream.
We had difficulty with this little black cat last week, but
this test requires only a small amount of blood to work

properly. Toxoplasmosis is a zoonotic malady and especially dangerous to pregnant women. Cats are often carriers of the disease but rarely become sick from it. Ozzie may be an exception to that rule. Protozoa contained in the cat's stool are the cause of toxoplasmosis, although it takes a good 24 hours to become infective once it's shed in the stool. People come into contact with it from cleaning litter boxes, but gardening in soil where cats have gone to the bathroom is an even more common occurrence. Doctors often draw blood from pregnant women to test for this disease, since it can affect the fetus. I was tested when pregnant with all three of my children and thankfully came up negative each time.

Surgery is finished by 11 o'clock and I leave the office to meet my husband for lunch. While we're eating I receive a page from a man who is a client of one of the other hospitals in the area. His dog has developed strange lumps all over his body. The dog is acting fine, but these lumps seemingly appeared out of nowhere just this morning. I offer to examine the dog at our office, but he decides to wait until two o'clock, when his regular veterinarian will be on duty. Emergency calls during lunch don't happen all that often. Given the opportunity to see us immediately or wait a couple of hours until their own clinic reopens, most people invariably choose the latter.

I return at four o'clock to attend the four appointments scheduled for late this afternoon. Dylan, Dolly, Juno, and Salo will all be seen for routing wellness exams and vaccinations. We're nearly finished when my pager sounds. The gentleman on the phone has three huskies he normally takes to a different clinic. Apparently one of his huskies attacked another and ripped off the tip of an ear. The ear is no longer bleeding, but there are a couple of other wounds on the dog. I offer to provide an evaluation but, with bite wounds, some form of surgery may be necessary. Since we won't be adequately staffed for surgery until morning, an advisory exam is about all I can provide. He elects to treat the dog at home with a weak Betadine solution and will call his regular veterinarian in the morning. Bite wounds, especially from other dogs, can be very serious. What you see on the surface is only a window to what may have taken place beneath the skin. Canine teeth are designed to rip and shred. When they puncture the skin, damage to underlying blood vessels often result. Bite wounds also tend to go deep into the muscle, which provides certain types of anaerobic bacteria a wonderful place to proliferate. Surgery is usually the recommended treatment, where Penrose drains can be placed at the wound site to allow fluid, pus and debris to drain away. These drains also serve as an entry point for flushing the wound with Betadine, which acts as a cleanser. The drains usually remain in place for three to five days, and the sutures will come out 10 days after that. Because the owner knew the vaccine status of the attacker as well as the victim, a rabies booster and quarantine is probably not necessary.

LESSONS/PROBLEMS

As the on-call veterinarian, I may hear from clients during my lunchtime and at all hours of the night. Sometimes emergencies can't wait until morning.

PREDICTIONS
- *Provide vaccinations to three dogs from the same family*
- *See two dogs with new lumps on their body*

DIARY
At 5:30 a.m. my pager goes off, waking me from a sound sleep. The caller is a client of one of the other veterinary clinics, and his dog has been in labor for two days. He tells me she produced one puppy two days ago but has been actively straining since eight o'clock last night. She's a chocolate Lab that typically produces 10 puppies to a litter. I explain that a puppy is quite likely stuck in the birth canal and an examination is strongly advised to see what's happening. Radiography is also warranted to see how many puppies might remain. For some reason he seems reluctant to drive the half hour to our hospital. I remind him that his own hospital will open at eight o'clock, but I'm not sure how much danger the mother is in if we wait that long. He also doesn't want to pay the emergency-treatment charge or the C-section fee, instead saying he'll wait until his own clinic opens for business. Before we hang up I say he's welcome to call me back if he changes his mind.

I'm often relieved that I don't have to go into the hospital whenever I receive emergency calls like this, but I'm also worried for the patient. Quite often I've found that so-called emergency calls are basically people looking for free

SURGERY PACKS AND SUTURE MATERIAL.

veterinary advice. Others want me to diagnose their pet over the phone, and still others refuse to pay any type of emergency fee. All I can do is offer to examine their animal at our clinic; the rest is up to them. Shortly after eight o'clock my curiosity gets the best of me. I call the clinic where the gentleman claims to go. Believe it or not, they have no record of him ever taking his dog there. I sure hope he found help somewhere.

My first appointment of the morning is a great client of ours who owns many animals. Today she brings in her three dogs for kennel cough vaccinations. With her children out of school she's headed south for vacation, and she wants to make sure her dogs are well prepared before they're boarded for the week. Then I see Jesse, a nine-year-old Labrador retriever. He's been drinking a lot of water lately and his owner fears he may have been licking salt off their driveway. I'm not convinced by that explanation, so we run some blood work and do a urinalysis to see what's going on. My main concerns involve diabetes, Cushing's disease, liver disease, or possible a urinary tract infection. All of Jesse's tests come back normal, but I see a few white blood cells in his urine. We elect to treat him with a round of antibiotics for now.

Ralph is my 11 o'clock appointment. I examined him a few weeks ago because of his considerable weight loss. His owners had reported he was vomiting up every meal he ate, but additional investigation caused me to believe he was actually regurgitating his food. Since nothing ever reached his stomach, he was not getting any nutrition. That's what apparently caused him to lose the weight. However, all this is pure speculation on my part since his owners declined any additional diagnostics. We managed to get some food into him over the past few weeks by feeding him in an upright position, but now he's doing poorly again and his owners decided they want to have him euthanized.

After lunch at home I return for my three afternoon appointments. This is our slow period of the year, which allows me to spend more time with my family but also affects my pocketbook, since the revenue we generate at the clinic helps determine the size of my paycheck. I have one vaccination scheduled and two lumps to check. Lumps can be difficult to evaluate by the naked eye. Benign and malignant skin tumors often look and feel the same. Whenever an owner notices a skin tumor, we recommend aspirating it with a needle to see if that tells us whether we're dealing with fatty tissue or something entirely different. Should this process fail to give us a clear answer, we have two remaining options. First we can watch it closely for any change in size or consistency. Second we can do a biopsy, which involves excising part of the lump and examining the cell structure for anything cancerous. The two dogs I see this afternoon have benign lumps known as lipomas, and no further action is necessary.

LESSONS/PROBLEMS

Emergencies can happen at all hours of the day or night, but many times I'm left wondering how much of an emergency it might have been if the owner chooses to take no further action. Drinking too much water can be an indication of any number of diseases, which means that further testing is almost always necessary.

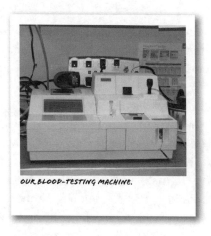
OUR BLOOD-TESTING MACHINE.

Day 26 *FEBRUARY 9*

PREDICTIONS
- *Examine a puppy having urinary accidents*
- *See a vomiting cat with a history of pancreatitis*

DIARY
This morning I have seven appointments, which is busier than I've been for the past few weeks. Most are routine exams, but my last two prove more complicated. The first of these is Emma, a beautiful Springer spaniel puppy who has been experiencing urinary accidents. Her owners are very nice people who give her all the attention and exercise she needs. We run a urinalysis and, sure enough, she has an infection. I place her on antibiotics and recommend we do another urinalysis in two weeks. Urinary tract infections can occur for many reasons. Sometimes it's because the pet is

not getting enough water, or perhaps they're asked to hold their urine for long periods of time. Dogs with arthritis can be victims of urinary tract infections, mainly because it hurts for them to sit in one position for any length of time and they fail to completely evacuate their bladder. Other animals have bladder stones that predispose them to infections. Sometimes there's a congenital reason, such as with an ectopic ureter. This is where the ureter—the duct that connect a kidney to the bladder—is attached somewhere other than the bladder. This condition is diagnosed with something called an IVP or renogram and can be repaired surgically. In this situation, the fact that Emma is built low to the ground and is also learning to become housebroken both contribute to her infection. If the infection returns or fails to go away with this first round of antibiotics, we'll look for other possible causes.

My final appointment this morning is Jebb, a new patient with a history of pancreatitis. This cat's owner states that he's vomiting again, as was the case when his former veterinarian diagnosed this condition. I mention other diagnostic tests, including blood work and radiography, to help rule out other possible reasons. However, the woman is convinced that her cat has pancreatitis once again and simply wants me to provide the medicine he took before. I give in and start him on Metronidazole. However, she needs it in liquid form since that's the only way she can get Jebb to ingest it. All we have on hand are pills and a tiny bit of liquid, so I send them home with a couple of doses and call in a prescription to a local compounding pharmacy for the rest.

She's happy with the outcome and agrees to bring him back for further diagnostics if he doesn't improve over the next 24 hours.

At 1:30 p.m. I return from lunch to perform another euthanasia. This time it's Sampson, an older dog I saw a few weeks ago due to his decrease in appetite and resulting weight loss. His blood work was consistent with kidney failure, but he wasn't vomiting at the time. Now he hasn't eaten much in several days and he has begun vomit up nearly everything he eats. He's also lost additional weight and has a certain sad look in his eyes. I recognize it's time to end his suffering.

At 7:00 p.m. I receive an emergency call from a very concerned dog owner. He tells me his pet was normal this morning but, following her evening walk, she began to stumble around. We agree to meet at the hospital. It's raining quite hard this evening, and Maine at night can be awfully dark where there are no streetlights. He apologizes for getting me out in such bad weather, but I explain it's all part of my job. The dog's exam reveals she has a head tilt and nystagmus, or rolling of the eyes. I look into one ear and see a great deal of debris. An ear smear reveals a bacterial infection and most likely a perforated eardrum, all of which are causing her neurological symptoms. I start her on eardrops that are supposed to be safe with ruptured eardrums as well as offering an anti-inflammatory solution. The owner will have his regular veterinarian check her again next week.

LESSONS/PROBLEMS

Even young puppies can get bladder infections. An inner ear infection can cause various neurological symptoms.

THE SCALE IN OUR WAITING ROOM WE USE FOR
WEIGHING LARGER DOGS.

Day 27 *FEBRUARY 10*

PREDICTIONS
- *Prepare for emergencies, as I'm on call this weekend*
- *Treat an older female dog that leaks urine and now has an infection*

DIARY
My on-call Saturday starts out slowly. Three of my four scheduled appointments are routine wellness exams and vaccinations, and the other is a possible urinary tract infection. Missy is a 15-year-old Lab mixture with a history of urinary leakage and ongoing bladder infections. We run a urinalysis, which uncovers bacteria and quite a few white blood cells in her urine. I start her on antibiotics and recommend a recheck in two weeks. Urine leakage is a

common problem with older spayed females, although it can be seen in younger dogs as well. When dogs are spayed, they lack sufficient estrogen to maintain good urinary sphincter tone. As a result, when the dog relaxes—especially when it's sleeping—urine will overpower the sphincter and leak out. Known as estrogen-induced incontinence, this condition can predispose dogs to bladder infections. We often put these dogs on a medication called Proin, whose generic name is phenylpropanalamine. This helps strengthen the sphincter muscle and thereby reduces the chance of leakage. If a dog is unresponsive to this medication, estrogen supplements can also be given. Because estrogen has more severe side effects, we avoid using it unless it's the only remaining solution.

I finished early with my scheduled patients and I'm home by 11 o'clock, which is quite unusual for a Saturday. However, close to 5:00 p.m. I hear from a distraught cat owner. Her pet came into the house a short while ago and seemed to have trouble walking. She'd first called her regular veterinarian, but their office was getting ready to close for the day. By the time we meet at our office, the cat appears to be walking without difficulty. The only thing I find during the exam is a luxating patella on the leg his owner says has been a problem. Since we're dealing with an older cat with a strong aversion to seeing the doctor, we run some blood work while they're there. I actually have some difficulty keeping the cat still enough to draw blood, so my husband comes in to help hold him. The blood test is normal. I send home instructions for his owner to watch him closely and call if he should come up limping again. At that point, our next step would involve radiography. A luxting patella is a condition where the kneecap isn't firmly seated on the knee joint. This can be a genetic defect or perhaps secondary consequences to an injury. We see this quite often in small dogs as well as cats. The situation rarely causes a problem unless the animal happens to gain weight, which would put additional stress on the joint. Over time, arthritis can take hold and the dog or cat may need to be treated with glucosamine plus an anti-inflammatory medication. In extreme cases, surgery is necessary.

At half past one in the morning my pager goes off again. This time it's a pet owner who is a client of a different clinic and lives about 40 minutes away. He and his wife were awakened by a loud noise and, when they went to check on their new kitten, they found it in their dog's mouth. The man was able to separate the two, but the kitten is bleeding from its nose and seems depressed. I recommend that he bring the cat in immediately. He objects to paying the emergency fee and tells me he just wants to euthanize the cat so it won't continue to suffer. I explain we don't do that without a proper evaluation, and still there would be an emergency fee. He asks what might happen if he waits until morning. Since I haven't examined the cat there's no way for me to know that, but I admit there could be life-threatening injuries to the brain or lungs. He declines to come in, choosing instead to take his chances and see what happens with the cat. He'll check with his regular vet in the morning. I hope the cat will be all right and implore him to call me back if he changes his mind. My pager remains silent the rest of the night.

LESSONS/PROBLEMS

Urinary tract infections can occur in older dogs because of their inability to empty their bladder fully, which is often a result of limited mobility from arthritis. Sometimes clients find it easier to bring in their animal during emergency hours rather than regular business hours. At that point we usually try to squeeze in as many diagnostics as possible.

PREDICTIONS

- *See an outdoor cat with a bite wound*
- *Try to collect urine from a dog with bladder infection symptoms*

DIARY

At nine o'clock, a client from one of the other hospitals pages me. Their 15-month-old Bichon has been vomiting over the past few days. Her owners are concerned because she continues to act lethargically and shows no interest in eating. Their regular veterinarian saw the dog yesterday, at which point he took some radiographs. Nothing appeared to be out of the norm. After bringing her in to see me, I palpate her abdomen and recognize it's causing the dog some pain. My recommendation is to repeat the radiographs, since a foreign body is still a possibility. These will occasionally reveal themselves in time when you look at gas patterns. Sometimes two radiographs on consecutive days need to be taken to see if the patterns have changed. If not, a foreign body is suspected. However, the owners are hesitant to proceed. I don't know if it's for financial reasons or if they don't want to let the dog out of their sight, since it's obvious they're very attached to her. I finally get them to agree to let me run some blood work. The test comes back fine except for some mild electrolytic abnormalities. Because of that, I suggest we keep her in the hospital for a few hours on IV fluids, but they don't want to leave her. As a compromise I

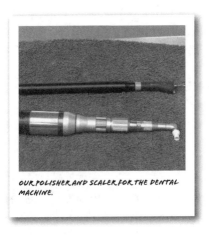

OUR POLISHER AND SCALER FOR THE DENTAL MACHINE.

administer some fluids under her skin and send them home. They agree to page me if her condition worsens today, and they'll visit their regular vet again tomorrow.

As I'm finishing up my first emergency, the pager goes off twice more. The first call is from an elderly woman whose cat came back into her house with bite wounds on his legs and a scratch above one eye. Shadow's owner is not feeling particularly well herself, so she asks if the cat can board with us for a few days while we treat his wounds. I agree to this arrangement. I'm able to flush his wounds, provide him with a rabies booster, and start his antibiotics before setting him up in surgery. Tomorrow we'll move him to one of our cat "condos" for boarding. The other emergency call comes from a client at another hospital. Their dog has been ill for a long time and now is unable to walk. The owners came to the conclusion this morning that the best way to ease their pet's suffering was to euthanize him. I tell them they're welcome to see me today, but they refuse because they want to wait and go to their regular vet in the morning. Apparently they assumed I'd be able to schedule the appointment for them, but I explain our two facilities are not connected. That means I don't have online access to their hospital's appointment network. They decide to call their regular provider in the morning.

After going home, my son and I decide to go over to the YMCA for a walk. This place is in the next town over, so it takes us about 20 minutes to get there. However, it's only 10 minutes from the hospital if something comes up, which means I can get there just as quickly as if I was at home. While we're walking around the track, I get a page from a client whose one-year-old pit bull started urinating blood this afternoon. The dog appears to be quite uncomfortable. I explain that a urinary tract infection may be uncomfortable, but it's rarely an emergency. They insist that I see her, so we agree to meet at the clinic in 30 minutes. This gives me time to take a few more laps before my son and I leave for the hospital, where we meet the client at five o'clock. I'm unable to obtain a urine sample from the dog, which will occasionally happen with very nervous and private animals. They're often uncomfortable about having someone hang around behind them with a dish, poised to jump down and catch the urine as soon as they squat. I provide some antibiotics but tell the owners not to start them until they get some urine out of her. They'll try tonight to accomplish this and will take the urine to their regular vet in the morning. I tell them to stick it in the refrigerator to keep it fresh, in case they collect a sample later this evening.

LESSONS/PROBLEMS

Sometimes it's easier for a person to board their animal than it is for them to treat it on their own. Regional emergency duty is often a collaborative effort, where multiple clinics in the area team up to keep the local pet population healthy.

OUR REFRIGERATOR FULL OF VACCINES.

Day 29 *FEBRUARY 12*

PREDICTIONS
- *See two ADRs in the morning*
- *Perform emergency surgery in the middle of the day*
- *Meet a cute puppy being trained to hunt*

DIARY
My three appointments are routine vaccinations, but my first ADR—Ain't Doin' Right—is an overweight cat the owner swears has had trouble breathing for years. The animal has been to three other veterinarians without receiving a definitive diagnosis. I find the woman to be quite a character in her own right. She's not easy to talk to because she doesn't listen well, and she shows classic signs of panic. During my exam, I confirm her worst fears because I find

a growth in the cat's right nostril. She demands that I use my forceps to remove it immediately, with the cat awake and alert. First I explain we can't possibly know what the mass may be without a biopsy, plus I'm hesitant to remove something like this without anesthesia. I don't want to risk further damage if excessive bleeding complicates the situation once I'm in there. I convince her to let me anesthetize her cat tomorrow and remove it then. She won't leave the cat in a cage, so she'll sit in the waiting room with it until it's time for her surgery, and also during the recovery process. I tell her to bring a book to read, since she may have a long wait.

My next ADR is a young cat that has been vomiting for the past three days. She's also bleeding from her vulva, and I find her dehydrated and depressed during her exam. Because she's never been spayed, I'm worried about pyometra. This is an infection with a potentially fatal outcome. The uterus fills up with pus and bacteria, which makes its way into the bloodstream and can result in infection, septic shock, and possibly multi-organ shutdown. The only treatment is to operate immediately and remove the infected uterus. Pyometra occurs in unspayed adult females, usually one to two months after their last heat. It's estimated that up to seventy percent of unspayed females will develop this life-threatening condition at some point in their lives, which is a strong argument for early spaying of your dog or cat. Scrappy's radiographs are consistent with pyometra and her blood work is normal except for a mild dehydration. My colleague has another surgery scheduled for 11 o'clock, so this patient will have to wait until 1:00 p.m. I return to the clinic after lunch to find that my assistant inserted an IV catheter and has already started fluids. We prep Scrappy for surgery and then I scrub up. When I enter her abdomen, the infection is much worse that I thought. I see evidence of disease on all the organs that touch the uterus including the omentum, which is a fold of the peritoneum that attaches to the stomach. I'm able to remove the uterus without causing any leakage, so chances are good she'll be all right. We'll keep her overnight on fluid therapy and send her home tomorrow on antibiotics.

I finish surgery just in time to look after my three afternoon appointments. This afternoon I have two routine wellness exams and vaccinations, finishing with someone new. Our new patient is a cute five-month-old German shorthaired pointer given to her owner as a bird-hunting partner. He tells me he's never trained a dog to hunt birds, but he has all the resources to learn and is looking forward to their many adventures together. After leaving the hospital at five o'clock, I return two hours later to check on Scrappy. She's doing much better and seems brighter, although she's not interested in food just yet. I give her a pain injection and check her fluids. Then I shut off the light so she can settle down for the night.

LESSONS/PROBLEMS
It is important to spay your female cats and dogs because they are otherwise at risk for pyometra, which can be a life-threatening condition.

THE BULLETIN BOARD IN THE VESTIBULE,
WHERE PEOPLE PLACE ADS FOR ANYTHING
FROM PUPPIES AND KITTENS FOR SALE TO
GROOMING SERVICES OFFERED.

Day 30 FEBRUARY 13

PREDICTIONS

- *Neuter a cryptorchid German shepherd*
- *Diagnose a nasal tumor in a cat*
- *Shave matted hair on an old cat*

DIARY

My first patient today is J.B., a German shepherd suffering from cryptorchidism. This means one of his testicles has not descended into the scrotum. As male dogs mature the testicles travel from the abdomen, through the inguinal ring, and then into the scrotal sac. This usually occurs by the time the dog is four months old. In this dog's case, it hasn't happened yet and he's already six months old. Because I can't feel the testicle upon palpation, I'm forced to open up

MY WORK SPACE.

his abdomen and find it. The surgery is more labor-intensive than regular castration, plus it's more painful for the dog. While we have him under anesthesia we'll radiograph his hips, because his owner reports he's had difficulty standing up after lying prone on a linoleum floor.

While J.B. is prepared for surgery I begin to operate on Daisy the cat, whose owner wouldn't leave her in the hospital and plans to sit in our waiting room. We anesthetize the feline, which allows me to get a better look down her throat. Nasal polyps can occasionally be seen at the back of the throat and even removed from there with steady traction. I don't see any evidence of a polyp in the back of her throat, so I decide to pull on the tumor directly from her nose. It breaks away and begins to bleed. We're able to control the bleeding, but I'm concerned there is more to this tumor than meets the eye. I speak to Daisy's owner and provide her with several

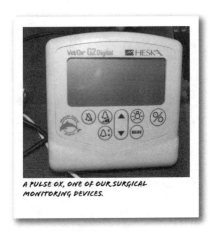

A PULSE OX, ONE OF OUR SURGICAL MONITORING DEVICES.

options. We could send the cat out for more diagnostics to place an endoscope in her nose, or perform a radiograph to see how extensive the tumor is, or I could try and remove more of the material, and biopsy it. She decides to wake the cat up and take her home until she shows signs of discomfort at some future time.

J.B. is next on my list. First I explore his abdomen, finding his testicle hidden up near his bladder. After removing the undescended one, I remove his normal testicle as well. The result of all this work will be a fairly large incision to heal. After surgery, we radiograph him. His hips are not seated well in their sockets, the spot known on the body as the acetabulum. I expect this condition will lead to arthritis over time. I call his owner and fill him in on the situation.

After J.B., we begin to tackle our dentals. First up is Jojo, who

I saw a few weeks ago. His dental is pretty straightforward and we're finished in practically no time at all. The second dental, Nikki, is not terribly happy about being in the hospital. He lunges and swats at us while we're trying to remove him from the cage. I'm finally able to grab him by wearing gloves and draping a towel over his head before putting him into the anesthesia chamber. His teeth are in fairly good shape and we place him in his carrier to wake up, since he's such a pain to handle.

While I'm helping with Nikki's teeth, the technicians are shaving the mats on Annie the cat. Longhairs will occasionally develop deeply tangled hair if they're not groomed regularly. Elderly cats in particular find it difficult to self-groom, especially if arthritis prevents them from reaching every possible surface. Many times the only solution to eliminating these clumps of hair is to shave them off, which is what we're doing to Annie. She doesn't like us very much, but at least we're able to remove most of her mats.

I return to the office at four o'clock to do a few vaccinations, finishing up by seven. At midnight I get a call from one of our clients. Her one-year-old Saint Bernard is acting strangely. She thinks she may be bloating. The owner describes some of the classic signs of bloat but tells me the dog seems much more comfortable now that she's burped. I give her the option of coming in as an emergency, but she decides to keep watch for now and will call back if the dog fails to improve overnight.

LESSONS/PROBLEMS

Sometime treating the owner is just as important as treating the patient. Dogs that are cryptorchid should be neutered. Sometimes cats can be difficult to handle. Bloat is a life-threatening condition that occurs in dogs with deep chests.